Secrets of the Sales Master

Secrets of the Sales Master

One Mans Mission To Share His Secrets

Craig Faulkner

Secrets of the Sales Master

For Jasmin, Poppy-Alice & Abbie

Your love is what drives me to give 100%

Introduction

Welcome to *'Secrets of a Sales Master'* this book is your one stop guide to taking yourself to the next level in sales, and the next level and the one after that. Congratulations on taking step one, that's right you are now already participating in the promotion of your career. By which I mean, that by having purchased this book you have made the conscious decision to improve your approach to sales, and for that I applaud you. We can now collectively allow ourselves to move on to what makes me, Craig Faulkner, the sales master that you wish to emulate. Moreover, how it is I can pass this very real talent of selling onto you, which will then enable you to determine your own destiny in the world of sales.

Ladies and Gentlemen allow me to introduce to you; the very real secrets of a sales masters. Whatever your age; young, old somewhere between. If you have none or many years of experience. What I have discovered during my career in sales is; I learn something relevant and completely new every single day. I appreciate that everyday something will be developed in my strategy that will improve my performance. It could be anything, whether it is how I am currently booking my appointments, altering the way I speak, changing my eye movements, all the way through to closing the sale, I always, always learn something new. Moreover in every single training session I have attended I have adjusted at least one of the elements of the way I play my game to ensure that I can achieve a minimum extra sale each day!

And so it begins; now it is my belief that every human being on the planet is involved in a sale of some kind or another. And, I'll explain to you why. From the 'closing a Multi-million dollar deal' to 'selling the idea of a visit to a shopping arcade, on to your other half' every single conversation we have, whether it be a spouse, friend, family member, colleague or business partner, a sale is involved.

The questions we find ourselves asking at this juncture are: what is to come of this myriad of sales we find ourselves embroiled in daily? How do we, Joe Bloggs, control our own destiny and ensure that each and every sale in our selling infused existence has the same injection of energy, combination of skill and ultimately the same outcome, we win it! Well, this book is designed to teach you how the art of influence, accompanied by control and direction, may change how you deal with your selling opportunities. This book will allow you to know the outcome of every sale to the point where, you can accurately predict your client's response before they themselves know what they have decided. It will teach you how to be in tune with your clients and to understand their emotional relationship to the product you are offering to them. It will put you in line with your client's 'Wavelength' which can enable you to build an unbreakable and lasting rapport with them, something that can never be overused. Finally, this book will show you how you will maintain a positive attitude in the face of adversity, how you will ignore the negative stances even when they come from the ones closest to you, and in doing so you will be sure to increase the turnover in your sales which in turn will make your bank manager your best friend.

So the first thing I might ask, if I were you, why is this book important to me? My educated guess is that you feel that you would like to earn more money and achieve a higher level of performance in sales. Obviously, but also allow you to look at yourself in the mirror each morning knowing you are filled with integrity and honour. Well, this book will get you there. By looking at sales from a different angle, in a different light and by changing your perspective on the things you feel you know like the back of your hand, along with taking your mind set from my work to my pleasure.

So, let me ask only one thing of you; just read a chapter a day. Then once you have completed the book, go back, and read from the start again. But this next time read two chapters a day. Then do it all again a third time, but this time read the entire book cover to cover over the period of a weekend. That is a tall order I know, that is not too much to ask, is it? But if you do, I will promise you this much; within two months your sales figures will explode. I guarantee, yes guarantee that you will be working less hours and making more money. OR' better yet working longer hours, simply because you now love what you do. And let us not forget you will be making an absolute fortune.

Secrets of a Sales Master, will become your doctrine. It will be the first thing you read in the morning and the last thing to read at night. Throughout this book you will see there is a step by step guide in implementing these valuable techniques. My friend I say to you only this, stick to what I share with you and one day I will share with you the story of how this book was the pivotal point in your life, where you became a sales master. One day I hope to shake your hand and congratulate you on achieving your goals. After all that's my dream now as well as yours.

One interesting thing I have come to understand about all of us is, regardless of what each individual (you) believes about their current ability, they will have a flair or specific ability with something, a minimum single aspect of their sale. There will be elements of their sales process that they are great at. Granted, other areas may need to be improved but there will be something within the process that they are already accomplished in.

In order to change the elements of each individual's sales process, so that they thrive in all aspects of their pitch I have over the years developed this book in order to open their eyes to an entirely different style of selling. A style that only the top 1% of sales professionals, are currently using during their sales process, and in doing so, are working in a profoundly conscious level of self development, and awareness, in a small utterly professional field. This book will enlighten the reader and enable them to increase their income exponentially. The readers of this book will become so influenced by the information which I can share with them that it will transform their primal attributes and transform them into selling machines.

Moreover regardless of you being an employee, employer, one man sales initiative or million dollar entrepreneur this book will improve your quality of life and the influence that you can make in all aspects of your interactions with other people. You can use the tools I'm going to share with you to get whatever you need from life, and literally all it takes is ***Your Commitment to This Publication!***

I vehemently urge you to implement what I am about to share with you wholeheartedly for the next sixty days and you will be rooted to your new selling expertise, you will be transformed by how you deal with selling and you will categorically notice the positive upward transformation in yourself and in your sales targets.

This book should take you no more than a day to read. But, read it more than once. If there is a particular area that you don't understand, read it again. And again. Research it! Study it, Practise what it says, but most importantly do this one thing; Make yourself the promise that you will give it all you have got to give. Commit to the book, and the book will not steer you wrong. And if you give this book absolutely everything that you have got in the tank for the next sixty days, this book WILL give you everything you need to become that absolute sales master.

Chapter 1 –

Knowing who you are.

A vital element to knowing who you are is your ability to be honest with yourself. The telling of white lies to those whom you converse with is your business. But the more you choose to immerse yourself in a dishonest lifestyle the more likely you are to be consumed with your own dishonesty. The choices you make regarding truths may damage your belief in yourself, and your belief in your ability. Unfortunately there is no happy ending here, it is simply career suicide.

Instead let us allow ourselves to be honest here. Let us face the facts about who we are. Where are you? What are your finances like? What is your relationship status, and is it happy? What is your fashion? How tidy is your home? Are you proud of yourself? Are your family, more importantly, your children proud of you? Are you constantly borrowing money, and hardly ever paying it back? Are you trying to survive on a basic wage? Is that because you can never hit your targets to get commission? Or, are you doing ok, but feel you need that kick to take you up a couple of gears? Or better, are you *very* successful with your sales figures and your finances but you still don't feel completely fulfilled? So, with all that to ponder over and digest allow me to help you deal with your negative thoughts, before we tackle the skills of a sale.

In this section we need complete honesty, be truthful. Because it is just you and me, I can assure you that what happens here will go, absolutely, definitely, certainly no further. But seriously, if you are economical with the truth, at this juncture the entire book will be a lie for you. The truth is that; you do not have to share your personal details with me. I am for all intents a

Secrets of the Sales Master

purposes a hologram. I am an emotionless guide who is not here to judge, and this person, has no idea what you are writing down. What you write will be for your eyes only, but it really is a fantastic tool for you to see what your answers are in black and white. Allow them to sink in, and be honest with yourself.

Answer the following questions:

- How old are you?
- Is your relationship healthy?
- Is your family proud of you?
- What is the value of your savings, and are your bills all paid?
- Are you proud of yourself?
- Are you being honest??
- Do you argue with your spouse a lot?
- Are you often frustrated?
- Do you borrow money from people?
- Do you enjoy what you do to earn money?
- Do you have any written goals?
- Have you ever achieved a goal?
- Can you afford a holiday, today?
- Do you feel let down when you lose?
- Do you play to win or just to have fun?
- Do you tell white lies to friends and family?
- If you continue as you are, where will you be in twelve months?
- Do you read books, or listen to audio books?
- How many hours a week do you spend on your own development?
- Do you have any enemies?
- Do you avoid confrontation?
- Are you definitely answering all of these questions 100% truthfully?

Secrets of the Sales Master

These answers need to be written down and completed in private, behind a closed door. Do not discuss any of your thoughts with others. You must really contemplate your answers and exercise extreme honesty. Then just write the answers down. After you have done that the next step is to write a statement, just a short paragraph, but detailed, as to why you have chosen and written each specific answer. Once you have done that, keep all this information somewhere safe, it is for you to return to in the future. Remember you must be totally open and honest, you are learning about who you are, it is certainly most important to get it right. If you cannot trust yourself to be honest with you, who can you trust? You must trust you!

In order to achieve change we need to understand completely who and moreover where we are right now. By becoming involved in just one lie, you will be indulging a dishonest persona. This person is not you and can never be you. This persona will simply hold YOU back from becoming all that YOU can be. Someone else will be standing in the way of you achieving your potential, and that someone will be the lie. This version of you is not your whole truth. HE can't win! HE cannot be all that you can be, because he is not YOU. He has no potential!

The proof of this is of course in the witnessing. My own personal experience of lies, or rather liars is quite simple. An 'All Mouth Salesman' may walk into a new sales position. A position which; has been generated for him by using a web of lies, and a sense of misguided over-confidence which is without merit. However, he got the job. Job done, or so he thinks. He continues to walk proud, for all of a week. Then 'Mr. Nobody' falls flat on his face. He misses his targets, and loses his job. Why? It's simple, he doesn't exist. 'Mr. Nobody' is all lies, the guy behind those lies, can't tell the truth, and is incapable of truth. He can't be honest. He does not know who he is. What is more alarming is how easy it is to spot the ones who will fail; everyone just knows instantly. They are the ones who lie to themselves about who they are. All of the questions above that you have answered honestly they cannot, to them all their responses will be lies. So to those people I ask; why do that to yourself? Just be honest. Because with an honest person I can help make progress and then help make them money. So allow that to be, you and me. Let us be totally honest, together let us both make some money together.

You will need to spend at the very least two hours on this section, completing these questions. It is really that important, a true foundation. In doing so, you will have uncovered a truly enormous amount of very useful information about yourself. A great deal, I presume that you will be really proud about. Others perhaps not, maybe you have uncovered a little monster that we need to deal with. Embrace the monster; we will come back to it later in the book. Commit again now to the book, it will show you how to deal with the ugliest little monsters, and perhaps if we revisit the questions in twelve months' time, the information which you're are proud of will be the information about you that has control of your destiny.

Chapter 2 –

Knowing where to start.

By now you're going to have pretty good blueprint of your current position in life. Having answered the questions in the previous chapter we are now able to build on what we have learned. Firstly, there is no such thing as perfect! This is not opinion, it is fact 'Perfect' doesn't exist. Simply because there isn't anything that cannot be built upon and made better. You can always better your best. More importantly though, if you are low, and times are hard then we can certainly make significant improvements right here, right now.

To clarify I Craig Faulkner, I'm not a life coach! Oh, I am most definitely not! I do not aim to be, nor do I proclaim to be. What I am offering here is focused on improving your influence and selling skills. However, we need to understand why we are doing what we are doing. WE need to evaluate what money can do to improve that. Because no matter what your current position is in life, a little or a lot more money simply makes your problems seem less problematic. Right, let's get to work on you!

<u>Goals</u>:

I'm positive that there are elements of your past, things that you have achieved, that you are proud of. Whether it be competing or even winning in a race at sports day when you were a child, or appearing on television somehow or perhaps even the birth of a child. The next step that we need to take, is to make a list of at least five things in your life that you have personally achieved, and that you are proud of. Again brutal honesty is imperative. The calibre of achievement that we are now looking for is the type of thing, that by simply writing them down your shoulders seem higher, your smile is broader and your head is higher. Let this list make you smile like a Cheshire Cat. Allow your face to be hang from ear to ear with a jaw splitting grin, after all these are your highlights. Keep in mind as you do how others may feel about these achievements. Allow them to have an emotional connection to you. Achievements that if shared with another would somehow affect them. Would make them think about what you have done and maybe even melt their hearts a little.

What have you done that makes you feel proud:

1) _____
   _____
   _____

2) _____
   _____
   _____

3) _____
   _____
   _____

4) _____
   _____
   _____

5) _____
   _____
   _____

I dearly hope that you are gloating by now. You should be, we've just heard your best bits. Whilst you are revelling in the glory of your proud moments sink a little deeper into your mind, and ask yourself what made these achievements so wonderful? Why are these things important to me? Why these things, more than any other things and how do I really feel when I think about them? Using this information expand on what you have written and write a short paragraph about each of these memories. Explain how and why they are important, and what it is about them that fills you with pride?

1) Memory One is important to me because…

2) Memory Two is important to me because…

3) Memory Three is important to me because…

4) Memory Four is important to me because…

> 5) Memory Five is important to me because…

What do we now know about you? Well we know that you have the ability, potential and drive to make things happen. You have some pretty awesome memories. More than that, you have the determination and commitment to make things happen. To create moments in your life that makes you proud of you. All we have to do, it to train your own mind to create more awesomeness for you. Now is when we create a map for you, and in doing so, create your infinite ability to feel pride, and create more amazing moments in your life.

Secrets of the Sales Master

"Most people only work enough so that it feels like work, whereas successful people work at a pace that gets such satisfying results that work is a reward. Truly successful people don't even call it work; for them, it's a passion. Why? Because they do enough to win!"
   Grant Cardone

So let us get to it. The next task for you is to write down fifty things you would like to do before you shuffle off your mortal coil. Consider it a bucket list if you will. Your list can be as mundane or extravagant as you choose. Take your time with this. Google can be a great help, and you should research your goals. There will be some that you will know instantly, but there will also be some that you never knew were your goals. Think about your answers and allow your imagination to be your guide. It can be short term goals such as; buying a new suit for work, achieving an extra sale each week, a promotion at work, or perhaps spending time with a child or family member. Alternately of course you can think big and choose long term goals such as; climbing Mount Everest, Parachuting from a plane or achieving a seven figure sum in your bank. Maybe a mixture of both, but keep in mind that this is a dream list. Don't allow money or situations to be a factor. The sky is the limit, unless of course your goal is to take the Virgin galactic into space, then it's the stars for you. What I am trying to say is; open your mind. Allow yourself to dream big and ensure that your goals are what would really make that feeling you had during the memory task lift you into a new sphere of pride.

My Goals

1.	2.
3.	4.
5.	6.
7.	8.
9.	10.
11.	12.
13.	14.
15.	16.
17.	18.
19.	20.
21.	22.
23.	24.
25.	26.
27.	28.
29.	30.
31.	32.
33.	34.
35.	36.
37.	38.
39.	40.
41.	42.
43.	44.
45.	46.
47.	48.
49.	50.

Secrets of the Sales Master

Once you have completed your list. First take a break. It was a big list and hopefully you have put a lot of effort into writing it. After you've taken a break you need to revisit your list. As you look down your list please can you write a number next to each item? The number will be a representation of the amount of years that you feel it will take for you to achieve each goal.

Having done that, go through again and highlight all the goals that you feel you can achieve within one year. Of these yearlong goals choose four which you feel are the most important to you and write them down below, with a short paragraph about why they are important to you;

1	GOAL _____ IS IMPORTANT TO ME BECAUSE...
2	GOAL _____ IS IMPORTANT TO ME BECAUSE...
3	GOAL _____ IS IMPORTANT TO ME BECAUSE...
4	GOAL _____ IS IMPORTANT TO ME BECAUSE...

Secrets of the Sales Master

If you have been completely honest whilst writing out you goals, and you feel like there is an emotional attachment to them, the above four will pull you to achieving them. You may only complete three of them. But would you honestly deem that as failure? I know I wouldn't!

These four goals are to be looked at every day. If you have really targeted what makes you tick, then these goals will be all the motivation that you need. Hell, print the darn things out on a business card, laminate it, and put it in your wallet. Stick it next to your phone or computer screen. Take a picture of them and have them as the screen saver on your phone, and the desktop on your laptop. Make your life be about these goals. Eat, sleep and breathe completing your goals and be ruthless. Dreams don't make themselves come true.

The next item on the agenda is for you to consider the person that you need to become to achieve these goals. And for the love of god be honest. Ask yourself; if you were to knock on the door of opportunity, why would opportunity invite you in, to sit down and talk about your goals? Who is that person that opportunity may be interested in?

```
..........................................................
..........................................................
..........................................................
..........................................................
..........................................................
..........................................................
..........................................................
..........................................................
..........................................................
..........................................................
..........................................................
..........................................................
..........................................................
..........................................................
..........................................................
..........................................................
..........................................................
..........................................................
..........................................................
..........................................................
..........................................................
..........................................................
..........................................................
..........................................................
..........................................................
..........................................................
..........................................................
..........................................................
..........................................................
..........................................................
```

For a goal to be a driving force behind a ruthless mind there must be an emotional attachment to the goal in question. Some things just are not compelling enough to ensure you do not lose your focus. These things may be nice, but they are not goals. If whilst writing your goals in this section you haven't felt propelled forward by the desire to achieve them, then they are not a compelling enough focus for you. So you need to go back. Redo this section and think about the things that really excite you. Think about feelings that motivate you. Think again about your past achievement and really identify what it was about them that made you so darn proud of yourself. Find your driving force and use it. You need to lock in to what it is that makes you tick, and only then can you mould yourself into being the goal achiever that I know you are.

Chapter 3 –

Knowing what to expect

Okay so I know who I'm talking to here, I know you've been there, and I have been there too. It has been the cutting of our teeth hasn't it? Those negative customers I mean: the angry man or woman that is bold enough to simply tell you to 'fuck off', the hundreds of answering machines you get to talk to daily, unanswered calls on the phone, or the twitching curtains of the ones that can't even be bothered to tell you 'no', the horrible weather, the pen that just won't work, the other half giving you a hard time at home, the landlords that want to evict you because you are behind on your rent, the credit card companies that are sending red letters to your door, and now its 7pm and you're still on a doughnut, all part and parcel I'm afraid! Some of you know what I mean, we have lived it, I myself have had to negotiate terms with my wife and explain how 'it will pay off one day, I promise'. I too have had the bank manager send me payment reminders. And, I have even had zero sales at 7pm whilst sat there doubting myself.

But do you want to know something? I dealt with everything that was thrown at me. More than that, I am here now as a different, more productive, more grateful man. Would you like to know what turned me into a sales master, from the other guy that I used to be? I read a book! Just a book, granted it was a fantastic book. The book had the following extract:

'[...] you can't control traffic, weather, angry employees or anything like that, but the one thing you can control is the decision you make by what you see, hear or experience'
(Unsighted, 2015)

This sentence stood out to me more than anything I had previous read or heard. It resonated so profoundly with me that it made me look at other books searching for similar inspiration. But its true isn't it? If I were to throw a bucket of water at you, what would your brain tell you to do? I'm assuming that it would be along the lines of 'move!' Of course you don't want to get wet. You can't do anything about me throwing the water in the first place. It is quite simply out of your control. But you can move out of the way and prevent yourself from getting soaked, right? Well, sales are exactly the same. You can't control the fact someone wants to tell you to fuck off and close the door in your face. What you can control is how you react and deal with it. You can either allow it to get you down and take that emotion with you to the next house. Whereby it will directly affect the way the next house responds to you. Or, you could react differently. You could forget this negative person, and instead go to the next house as if it is your first call of the day. You could plaster that killer smile back on your face. You could hold your shoulders high and exhibit your profound confidence in your product and you can knock on the next door with pride. Similarly when your husband or wife is exacerbated at the bills and is threatening to leave you. Instead of screaming back about how they don't support you. Smile and explain to them that something big is going to happen, you know it. Hold them tightly and tell them that you love them and that you're in it together. When your creditors are sending you demanding letters, tell yourself that it is time for a pay rise, get out in the field and give yourself that pay rise by closing more sales than you have ever closed before.

When the WHY is big enough, we that are hungry can do anything! It is easy for me to write this, I'm in a position of having achieved my goals. Similarly it is easy for you to understand the notion of what I am attempting to convey. But, is it as easy for you to do? Is it simple for you to put yourself forward and attempt what I am asking you to do? Well yes actually it is! It really is that simple all you have to do is to decide to do it. That's right simply say to yourself right now, I can just decide to be more positive, I can simply decide to be better at sales, I can simply decide that things are better for me now, and believe yourself. You decided to buy this book because are a believer. You believe that this book can help you. You are right of course, this book can help you. There would be little point in me sitting here for hours on end writing this book, if its end game wasn't to provide you with the solutions that I have discovered. So to make this book work, let us use it right. Let us take the information that is being imparted and implement it into a more productive life style. Its not just possible for you to just do it, it is actually impossible for you to not achieve your goals if you follow this guide!

That's the negative out the way, so let's explore deeper on what we must expect on the day to day activity of sales:

Law of Averages – It's a numbers game

You know it has been eye opening to me the sheer number of individuals who simply give up on sales in their first week. Well of course there are numerous reasons why different people may decide that the life of sales is not for them. But my experience has shown me, that the number one reason why so many wannabe sales representatives have bit the dust in week one is numbers! That's right ladies and gentlemen. When some new up and coming personality enters the world of sales, they expect to be able to sell snow to the Eskimos in week one. They expect every single phone call to be greeted by Rockefeller ready to hand over his hard earned cash to their every whim. Wrong! It doesn't work like that, does it? We know, we've been there! After call seven hundred and twenty eight you may be lucky enough to get through to a person, rather than an answering machine.

> *"I find that the harder I work, the more luck I seem to have"*
> Thomas Jefferson

As fresh meat in the selling arena you should expect a bumpy start. Whether you're a wet behind the ears complete newbie, or a cultured seller in a new role it's important to remember that hardly anyone ever gets off to a flying start, by smashing all their targets in week one. It is just not done. The reason for this is you're just finding your feet. You should spend these first precious weeks getting to know your product inside out (you'll need this information later). Yes the first weeks are about familiarising oneself with a new selling environment, adjusting to new boundaries and compliance etc. And this is why I am always so bemused by those who simply walk away in week one. What could they possibly know of their future in sales by working out how the fax machine works, and locating the kitchen for a cup of tea? I understand that they may see the long term sales masters of the office smashing targets and breaking records, but they knew where the kettle was years ago! Seriously, do these new faces actually expect to be trading blows with the office big guns? Apparently so! For me it is unfathomable, until your felt your feet for a while you can't perfect your pitch, and get into your flow. So this is my message to any newbie sales people who are reading this: if you are in a new sales position and you are not breaking any records, keep going! But here is a little trick for you: *dial faster or knock longer.* The truth is you need to pitch more people until you have a finely tuned pitch.

It is a fact I promise you, that until you can tune your pitch you can't improve those sales figures. And do you know something else, if anyone tells your anything different, I'm sorry to say they do not have your best interests at heart and are probably setting you up to fail. I've myself have done it. I have literally spent nights sat up perfecting my pitch. Considering it; learning your lines! You wouldn't haul your arse up onto a West End stage without perfecting your lines, well your pitch is your play, and you have to nail it, or the show will be a big old flop! So take it from me, who has had many of nights staying up (Not on purpose) pitching in my head over and over, hitting the phones earlier and staying in the office longer, until I was totally confident with my ability and my product knowledge. However be warned, do not fall into the trap of being too comfortable. Don't ever stop the dedication to improving your ability further.

"All progress takes place outside of the comfort zone"

I once worked for a Door-to-Door company, my word was that a challenge. Not for the sales, nor for the negative customers, but because I just didn't know what time of day I'd be getting a sale. I recall once working in Bury, a small town just outside Manchester; I started knocking on the doors at 10am. This one day it was cold, wet and windy, and by 6.30pm I was on zero sales. As you can probably imagine I had got my fair share of rejection that day. I had also had a lot of un-answered doors. My feet where blistered and sore. My clothing was so wet that I now had to walk slower down the road due to haul the excess weight now been carried by my water saturated clothing. I was, I don't deny it, at the point of throwing in the towel. I should add the disclaimer here that it was in fact my first year in sales. So feeling deflated, I made a phone call to my sales manager. I was ringing to tell him that it was not working out for me, and

I was going to call it a day. The following conversation occurred:

My Manager: "so you've knocked on all the doors in your area and spoke to say fifty people?"
Me: "yes"
My Manager: "and you have got no sales?
Me: "Yeah that's right, I haven't got any"
My Manager: "and now you want to throw the towel in?"
Me: "Yes" (me now sounding very exasperated with him)
My Manager: "fantastic! Let me come and meet you. I'll take your list of properties, and you can go home to your wife and tell her you are a failure. In the mean time I'll continue knocking in your area because I know you have got rid of all the negative bastards, which means there is are loads of sales coming. (He's now laughing) I've already made £300 today and I'd love to work your area and make £300 more"
Me: "Er no do you know what I'll just keep going a bit longer"
(Thinking to myself "Prick!")

Secrets of the Sales Master

But what was he getting at? It's simple, he knew that if I was to keep going someone eventually was going to say 'Yes, and he was right. Yes, by 9pm I went home £200 richer than I was less than three hours before. I just picked myself back up, started the day again (In my head) and smashed out three sales, and it's all because I kept going.

> *"The reasons those succeed when walking through the valley of the shadow of death, is because they have a vision of the other side."*
> *Jim Rohn*

When I first started, I didn't realise how important it was just to keep going, but now I don't let time affect me. My goals are too strong to allow time to get the better of me. I can talk about the 'Laws of Averages' all day long. But it is easy to understand, just keep doing what you are doing and results will eventually show. To understand the 'Laws of Averages' some more, try this test: Say you are on the phones and have one hundred numbers to ring. You ring one hundred numbers each day for five days, so that's five hundred numbers in total. Get a sheet of A4 paper and write the numbers from one to one hundred. Every time you make a call (Connected Call) cross off the lowest number. Once you get a sale, circle the lowest number and continue. What you will find that over the week is this, the evidence will highlight that you will get a sale at any time of the day. If you keep up the same pace, work the same hours and pitch in the same way. But what it will also show is, you don't know when the sales are going to come.

> *"A dream doesn't become reality through magic; it takes sweat, determination and hard work."*
> Colin Powell

Secrets of the Sales Master

Chapter 4 –

Knowing Your Product, and Knowing How to Sell Your Product

I was invited to consult with a company in Mumbai, India. For legal reasons I will keep this information vague. The meeting came around when I was approached by the owner of the business at a sales training event, and he requested the pleasure of my presence at his business to provide further training for his staff. This is something I have done frequently and was nothing out of the ordinary, so away I went. When I arrived at the company I was surprised to find that ninety minutes of the two hour meeting I spent in the reception area. Here I was regularly indulged with refreshments, but none the less kept waiting because the owners were too busy to see me, even though I was there at their request. Ironically this actually provided me with a deeper insight into the company than was later divulged to me by the owner in our thirty minute conversation.

After exchanging pleasantries and listening intently to what he felt were the issues in his company I explained what I had witnessed and what he would need to do to resolve the issues in his business. It went like this:

Owner: But Craig, I don't want to bother about issues A, B and C on the list. Let us just focus on issues D and E. I am positive that the other problems will take care of themselves.

Me: Well I wish you luck with that Mr. Owner, but you will need to move forward without my council as I will not being administering a kiddies plaster to a broken leg, and expecting it to heal.

Owner: What do you mean?

Me: It is simple really. Your employees do not have enough product knowledge. They don't know the product inside out, they don't have belief in the product, and that simply means that they do not know how to sell your product. What you are asking for cannot be done, as you are not willing to educate your employees about the product you want them to sell. And until you do want to, I will not be doing business with you.

Eventually, I ensured that the owner understood the mistakes he was making, He changed his attitude and together we changed his business. His employees were in the end delighted and not only did his sales increase but the staff turn around dropped, and employment retention grew to an all-time high. The point here is, it pays to know your business!

If you go by the title; Entrepreneur, you *will* have a serious amount of product knowledge. If the product you are promoting is not known to you like the back of your hand, you are not an entrepreneur! So too goes for, a salesman in a company. If this is you, then you need to research everything about your product. But I mean really know it, research the competitors, research market activity, research growing trends, and find out who are the major players. Seriously you need to know this. You need to know everything about your product to be completely sold yourself. Sold so much into what you are selling that other people will accept your belief and buy into you.

Check list:

- Tool number one; RESEARCH
- Tool number two; HOW TO SELL YOUR PRODUCT

At this juncture, please allow me to guide you through the world of; 'Neuro Linguistic Programming'. Or, NLP for short. A lot of apprehension is felt about this particular method of categorising people, but trust me it works. And, along with most of what I will show you in this book, NLP can also be used to influence anyone and everyone that you interact with.

Words

I assume that we all acknowledge that we have a preferred learning technique. Whether it is Visual, Auditory or Kinaesthetic we all have a specific preference to the way in which we ingest information and retain it. But, did you realise that we speak that way also?

We use all three modes in speech. However, there is one we use more than the others. To demonstrate this I am going to provide you with the following example: When talking to a visual person, we should use words such as; see, bright, light, view, look, perspective, picture etcetera. Similarly with an auditory person, we should use words such as; sound, hear, noise, ring a bell, heard, loud etcetera. Therefore it goes without saying that when speaking with a kinaesthetic person we should use words such as; feel, touch, hold, felt, grasp, and so on.

There is of course a reason for this, we all think in pictures. The words we use in everyday life are simply triggers for images that we have in our brains. They are representations of an image that causes us to connect with what is being said to us. To gain rapport with another individual then, we need to trigger the types of images that are important to them, hence NLP. We use their key words to build a relationship with someone and develop a likeminded understanding or mutual agreement.

It is therefore understandably important to establish how your prospect thinks. Or more importantly how they speak! The best way to do this is to listen. That's right, when you make first contact with your new lead listen to how he or she speaks. Pay close attention to his or her selection of words. As I have explained, we all use all three modes. But, there should be one that we use more often than the others. It is important to remember that if you are speaking to a kinaesthetic person (for example) and you use words which are more auditory, then it will take that person longer to translate those words into relevant images. Whereas if you use the words that they naturally associate with, the conversation will flow much smoother and the person will fully understand you. You are therefore going to pose yourself as a translator of the mind.

Make it your role to interpret language to suit your audience. By doing so the person whom you speak with will naturally connect with you and allow rapport to flourish. If a client on the other hand doesn't connect with you they are more likely to say: "I need to think about it!" This isn't the response you want, so have a think about these three questions, they all mean the same thing essentially but are asked in a way that represents an individual's preferred language:

- Visual - Do you see what I mean?

- Auditory - How does that sound?

- Kinaesthetic – What are your feelings about it?

Rapport

You can have all the product knowledge, and competitor intelligence available in the world. You can look and smell like a million dollars. However, if you do not know all the tools for building rapport, you may as well work in a library. Building rapport builds confidence. Rapport allows your customer to feel safe dealing with you. It provides them with a platform of comfort and belief in you. With this new gateway into your clients trust, you will be able to further explore their feelings and allow them to open up more to you. You will be able to collect more information to provide the right products and services. And, most importantly you will be able to close the deal.

"The toughest thing about the power of trust is that it's very difficult to build and very easy to destroy. The essence of trust building is to empathise the similarities between you and the customer"
Thomas J, Watson

Secrets of the Sales Master

There are a number of different techniques in building rapport. My advice to you is; use them all. Using all techniques or even just the ones you feel most comfortable with will increase your sales dramatically. Honestly, you could even be the number one salesman in your organisation right now. It really matters, if you're reading this, you want to do better. What I am about to share with you will take you up to a whole new level in sales! Conversely, if you are new to sales and just starting off, well trust me, implement the following and the rewards will come exponentially. I assure you, more than anything you can possibly imagine 'Rapport' is the essence of selling!

It is a common misconception that rapport can only be built with likeminded people. An attitude that is particularly prominent with the sales industry. As a direct result of this, sales people in general determine that creating relationships with people who are not likeminded is impossible. How wrong can they be? All they are doing is limiting the amount of people they can do business with. Why would anyone want to do that? As a sales person you have to be a Chameleon. You have to alter your personality, to suit that of your client. Every client, even this Arsehole! Yes it means from time to time you too will have to say 'arsehole' but that is building rapport guys, suck it up! What is more important is not to limit your faith in your own ability. You can be whoever you choose to be. Bring yourself into the role, and find a common connection with your clients. It is in you to do it!

> *"Many believe effective networking is done face-to-face, building rapport with someone by looking at them in the eye, leading to a solid connection and foundational trust"*
> *Raymond Arroyo*

Let us move away from the limitations of personality. It is my aspiration with this book to 'enable' all the people who read it. I want to help

Secrets of the Sales Master

every last one of you expand on your current abilities and develop new ways of identifying with your clients, all your clients. Allow me to help you take rapport to a new level. You see rapport is not just built upon asking questions. No it is far deeper than that, and although this may seem a difficult area to study, you actually have all the tools you need, so let us get started.

When we are asking questions of our customer, we do it to build up an understanding of who they are, what they want, and to look for something that we may have in common with them (to build rapport). However, what is important to understand is only 7% of our communication nuances, are words. That is a small number isn't it? But in all honesty as a race it's true that humans invariably do not listen to the words that they hear during conversations. Humans are actually very finely tuned to take other emotional triggers into consideration when communicating with others. Opinions about someone's words can be affected by: body language, tone of voice, breathing patterns, a verbal no etcetera. So it is most important to access the remaining 93% of your communication techniques.

Matching & Mirroring:

If you have been in sales for any length of time, you should be familiar with this notion. It's a well versed, and a well-rehearsed method of selling. Yes this is something that we do every single day of the week, every week of the year. We have all done it for our entire lives, but it's in the sales world where it is done on a conscious level. Matching & Mirroring is quite simply copying, **to a certain extent**, someone's posture, tone, mannerisms etcetera. The reason that we do this is to build rapport. Returning to what I was saying earlier, in sales you have to become a chameleon, and by matching and mirroring your client you are already buying into their psyche and becoming a likeminded person, or so they'll think. So allow me to break it down further, because matching and mirroring works. I'll take it point by point and provide you with a few tips as we go;

Tone of Voice:

Different levels of tone of voice create interest. Dislike, concern, hatred, empathy, lust, love are all characteristics that can be affected or demonstrated by tone of voice. I find that tone of voice can even turn you off, so much that you only see the lips moving. The tone of someone's voice can be so distracting that the words themselves lose all meaning.

Try this next phrase on your partner. Don't do it all in a short space of time, maybe different times of the day. But attempt to; each time you do say this, use a different tone, and listen and watch the reaction: "I love you" I'm assuming that when you say it softly, slowly and with real meaning you'll get the response you would ultimately expect after saying those three words.

Another way to adapt someone to align themselves with you is: If a prospective client is talking to you, but they are using a tone that makes you feel as if you do not have control, or that they are being overly aggressive, or just generally you're not comfortable with. Then copy it, obviously do it discretely and never be aggressive. But as you've adapted your tone to meet theirs slowly change it, and take control of the conversation and ultimately the customer. This will work in two completely different ways the first is the customer will unwittingly feel connected to you, although they will probably be unsure as to why. The second is you will now be dictating the tone of the conversation and you can bring it around to make you more comfortable and therefore more likely to make a sale.

An additional way to adapt a conversation that is uncomfortable is to take a deep breath. Ensure that the customer can hear you, and obviously this would work especially well during telephone conversations. Ensure that your tone is engineered to get the best response possible, and in case you were wondering, the response you desire is not just the answers to the questions you have asked. It is the response to the questions using the tone of your voice, and the way you sound as they answer you.

Speed

It is of course important to match the tone of your customer, but so too is it important to match the speed at which your customer speaks to you. You may have managed to match the tone of the customer perfectly, but if your pace is off then it is all for nought and you will be in trouble. The client is more likely to fall into tone with you, if you have fully matched both their tone and their speed of speech. And, matching the customer's pace will bring the customer inadvertently closer to you, it will gain rapport and build connections that your customer doesn't actually realise they are building. They will simply like you, without knowing why.

Metaphors

It is amazing how so many people choose poverty just by what they say and how they view money. Metaphors are a direct view at someone's feeling with regards to money and finances. Many times as a child I was taught phrases by parents, teachers or friends. Perhaps I never really thought about the implications of them, or whether or not they were in fact true. But somehow, I like many others, allowed myself to be programmed into believing them. Common metaphors that I have engaged with during conversations with clients include; Money doesn't grow on trees, Do you think I am made of money?, Is money burning a hole in your pocket?, The richer get richer, the poorer get poorer, A fool and his money are soon parted, and my particular favourite; Money is no object. Now because people are preconditioned to have specific feelings towards money, or the lack of it, they are able to give clues via common metaphors as to how they are feeling about you, and your pitch. By unlocking what it is, that each client is referring to, you will be able to circumnavigate the issue, and address the sale without the inaccurate views that a customer may have about what they can afford. Simply put, they can soon be encouraged to understand, that they cannot afford to not invest into you and/or your product.

'You don't see something until you have the right metaphor to let you perceive it'

Metaphors are a secret path to the inner workings of someones deepest thoughts. And if you listen closely, if someone is using a metaphor during a conversation it will inevitably be linked to either pain (this is fantastic for you) or pleasure. Now the way to use this to your advantage is to jot down any metaphors a customer may use during the conversation and then reword that metaphor later or, whilst removing the pain factor. Eg: "I'd love to invest but, I am saving for a "rainy day" Could be transformed into "rainy days will become a thing of the past, when you're living in eternal sunshine". By using the exact metaphor that the client has referred to, you are directly tapping into some under lying issue in the back of their mind. Furthermore, you have identified that issue subconsciously and explained to the client, that they needn't worry about it. Ultimately they will subconsciously think, you know what their troubles are, and that you are going to resolve them somehow. Obviously then, by eradicating the pain you have a greater chance of closing the sale.

Look out for a training on this on my website from September 2017

Posture

> *"Kids used to sit back and listen to lectures. Now they're leaning in. Body language has changed."*
> Mike Harvey

The way a person sits when they are speaking to you can unravel and highlight allot about how a person is feeling, and their natural personality. Inevitably if someone is nervous and wants to close themselves off from a conversation their posture can prevent commitment all by itself. If I person were to sit back, in their chair, perhaps with their arms folded it's an indication that they are physically closing themselves off from the conversation and being non-committal about what is being discussed. Conversely if a person leans forward and offers open hand gestures, they are directly engaging in the conversation. They are actively paying interest into what is being said, and more often than not they are genuinely interested in what is being said. It is of course rare that an individual will have trained themselves to hold their body in a specific way, but you can. Not only is it key to identifying how your clients feels about the conversation but you can actively demonstrate interest in your client simply by sitting in a specific way.

> *"My belief is that during conversations, it's not so much what you say, it's how you say it that matters. What's being heard is secondary to what's being seen, as body language leads the discussion and dictates the mood."*
> Jarod Kintz

Ninety-nine percent of the time your gut feelings of someone will be correct, and this is because you are naturally capable of reading their body language. So tap into this and exploit your natural abilities to ensure you are connecting with your client. A key to building rapport with your client is to again mirror their motions. I would advise that you do this subtly, as you will more than likely look foolish if you copy their every move. Don't make your movements clearly obvious but when you're with a prospect and they are sitting back in their chair with their arms folded, embrace that position yourself. But when they start to talk, purposely sit forward and really appear interested in what they are saying.

Take the time to study different people's posture and body language. Then if you know the person, compare their attributes to the way in which they hold themselves. You can learn so much about a person by their posture, and natural stance during conversations, and most of the time you don't even need to read a "how to" book about this, as a human you are naturally able to recognise signs that someone is either interested, not interested, bored, excited or even aroused by you simply by paying attention to how they move. Your human instincts will tell you all you need to know.

Gesture fits comfortably into this category and also identifies human emotions for the well trained sales executive to read at his or her leisure. As with posture, copying prospects gestures builds instant rapport. A gesture can be a simple and discreet movement, such as a click of the fingers, a wave of the hand, brushing of hair away from the face (although be careful with this one, its often a sign of attraction) But use them, these gestures are identifying someone's natural mannerisms, and to be in line with another to an extent where you move the same does generate a natural bond that is often underestimated. Head movements can be important also, when a customer is talking to you face to face, nod as though you understand, it shows you are interested and the customer will feel heard. By actively seeking to listen to your client, they will feel that their views are being respected and acknowledged.

"Deafness has left me acutely aware of both the duplicity that language is capable of and the many expressions the body cannot hide."

Terry Galloway

Facial Expressions

The average person will judge you within four seconds of meeting. They will judge how you hold yourself, how you dress, your walk and most importantly your facial expressions. Especially when you are meeting someone for the first time you need to wear a smile like you've just had morning sex and have eyes that wouldn't be out of place on the front cover of time magazine. That's right your facial expressions need to be perfect. Later on in your meeting that facial expression need to have transformed into an expression of sincere interest. If a client is talking to you, you need to look interested. Tilt your head to one side and focus your eyes upon them. Whatever you do, never look bored and do not yawn!

> *"The utmost form of respect is to give sincerely of your presence."*
> Mollie Marti

Eye Movements and Eye Contact

Natural human instinct will lead you straight here. Trust in yourself and allow your natural abilities to guide you. It is a commonly acknowledge instinct that allows you to know instantly when someone is lying to you. I have a lot of fun with my children here, as they honestly believe I can see through walls at the moment. But it is simple, I just know when I am being lied to, and you do too. That's right unless the person who you are speaking to is a very good liar (your spouse!) you should be able to read them. So, when they say something like I don't have the money, but they can't make eye contact with you. Remember all is not lost, this person is most definitely not short of a few bob, trust your gut, and remember you are in their company because they felt they had enough money to have the conversation with you face to face.

Another thing to remember is that eye contact is also directly related to thought modes, so visual, auditory and kinaesthetic persons will each have eye movements that relate to specific motions in their brain. By identifying what type of person you are dealing with you will be able to work out the following:

An average visual person will:

- o .Look up and to their right when they thinking about something that may happen in the future.
- o Look up and to their left when they are thinking about something that may have occurred in the past.

- And, if they have unfocused stare, they are probably converting words into images, to identify the meaning of them.

An average auditory person will:

- Look up and to their right when they are thinking about something that may happen in the future, similar to the average visual person.
- Look up and to their left when thinking something that may have occurred in the past.
- And, if they are looking down and to their left, they are more than likely converting words into sounds, for translation to their preferred medium.

And a kinaesthetic person will:

- Look down to their right when they are converting words into feelings to associate a connection with what is being said.

My own personal experiences of lies from customers has taught me that when someone is perhaps telling me a lie, that their eye movement is wider than usual. Their eyes often look defensive and erratic, and also the person may stutter a little during their speech as if their voice is not sure about the words which it conveys. Often, a deepening of their tone, or potentially faster speech is an indication of dishonesty. Or, sometimes a potential client may just take just a little longer to reply to a question. If an answer is natural it will come to the forefront of their minds immediately. So, if you feel like the answer came a second later than it should have done, then is fair to assume that person is potentially lying to you.

"What is the difference between an obstacle and an opportunity? Our attitude toward it. Every opportunity has a difficulty, and every difficulty has an opportunity."

Breathing Pattern

During telephone conversations, listening to someone's breathing patterns can be an efficient tell of how they are feeling about what is being said. The thing with a telephone conversation is, your other senses are removed. You cannot see the client to read any other tells, so the way they are breathing can be an insight to the missing information that could be obtained in a face to face meeting. Because you are in a blind state, all of your attention should be on their sounds, not just the sound of their voice, or what they are saying. However be sure it is every sign and missed breathe they make.

Some of the breathing patterns which are easily identified include: slow, deep breathing is an indication that the client may be worried about something, and the same goes for a client who is breathing very quickly. A sigh of relief is an indication that the client is satisfied about what has been discussed, whether it be the price or the product, something has made their breathing relax. This is an indication that it may be time to close the sale. A long breath may identify a customer who is not listening, which is obviously an indication that not enough rapport has been established, and therefore some work needs to be done to redress that situation.

Breathing patterns are not only for telephone conversations. During face to face engagements with clients you should strive to mirror a client's breathing pattern. We have touched on this before, and as I explained the symmetry of breathing between clients and sales executive unconsciously builds rapport.

Comfort circle

Everyone has their own specific proximity or comfort zone around them. It is a level of space between one individual and another that acts in similar way as a buffer zone, which makes that person feel relaxed if it is maintained. Invading a client's proximity zone is a catastrophic thing to do. It will immediately make them feel uncomfortable, and will destroy rapport. Standing too close to a client will instantly destroy rapport and make the client uncomfortable in your presence. However, standing too far away can be counterproductive as well, it says that you have something to hide, and that you aren't to be trusted. So you need to gauge the correct distance with each client, and ensure that rapport isn't destroyed by proximity.

The other side of this is, if the client invades your space, let them. I know, it will feel uncomfortable, but they are not trying to sell a product to you. Know that they are trying to interact with you on their own terms, and if allowing that person into your comfort zone, gets you another mark on the board and another pay cheque into the bank, suck it up buttercup! If that is what they need to build rapport it is certainly worth the discomfort on your behalf.

> *"I do not believe in taking the right decision, I take a decision and make it right."*
> *Muhammad Ali Jinnah*

Touch

From a firm handshake to a gentle tap on the back touch is a connection with a client which solidifies rapport. If you are able to converse with a client which culminates in physical interaction on this level, you have successfully built rapport. The handshake generates an instant connection, either you take control of the situation, or your prospect does. A firm handshake which is evenly matched generally means that you customer will go toe to toe with you, but is willing to listen to what you have to say, and if they are willing to listen to what you have to say and offer, they may be willing to buy into what you have to offer, providing you tick all of their boxes.

When shaking a person's hand, I have identified the following: If the client slightly tilts my hand to the right, the customer is telling me that they are in control. To replace their control with your own at this juncture, you should place your left hand on top of the hand shake. You have now told the customer 'now I'm in control. If you want to take control from the offset then simply tilt your hand to the left during that initial handshake.

Visual and auditory people are not necessarily disposed to more intrusive interactions such as the touch on the shoulder etcetera. This is mainly for the kinaesthetic type of individuals. However, in the case of the kinaesthetic person, a gentle touch on the should as an act of encouragement or of congratulations, at the right time, solidifies a relationship which will mean they will always come back to you, and never buy from anyone else.

Hand Movement

Right back as far as the patristic period of early Christianity it was commonly accepted the importance of allowing someone to see the palms of your hands during interactions, because it generates trust. That is why now today's Christians, Jews and Muslims prostate themselves to god, showing him their palms. It is to demonstrate to their god, that they have nothing to hide from him, and they speak the truth. As with metaphor, deeply ingrained impressions like that are passed on through generations, So much so, that now it is felt by all, almost unconsciously that the sight of someone's palms, is an indication of trust. It has mainly lost its religious connotations nowadays and is merely an unconscious act of openness.

It is amazing to think that the palm of your hand or at least the direction you hold it in facilitates the building of rapport. It's simple, by keeping the palm of your hands faced down, you are indicating to the person that you are a closed person, or have something to hide. Therefore, showing the palm of your hands to customers will make them feel as if you are being completely open with them. It is also important to recognise that using your hand to make gestures, such as pointing, means you are running the risk of pressuring any prospective clients. So guard away from direct, *unnecessary* pointing. This is not to say that you cannot use your hand to indicate a point or an idea that you need to speak about. But use a pointed finger sparingly, and never direct a pointed finger towards a client directly.

Empathy

My final device regarding rapport building is; Empathy. To be able to relate to a customer's situation is so important. Ensure that your customers each feel like you are the same as them, or at least you have been in similar situations in the past. Make it clear that you understand their circumstances and that you have felt the same way they do. Relating to a customer's circumstance has always been an excellent way to build rapport. But obviously, do it within reason. Never try to overshadow their tales of woe with more extravagant tales of your own. Still, allow them to know that you understand them, and have had similar life experiences.

It is quite a considerable list of techniques isn't it? There are plenty more ways to boot. Use as many techniques as is possible, but perhaps without morphing into your clients, like a sales chameleon. But use them during the correct circumstances and witness as your sales numbers dramatically increase.

The last thing I would ask you to consider is your product. If you feel that you are not selling a product that you are committed to and completely believe in, change it. Find something that you are sold on. If you would buy it, it is more honest to sell that product on to others. You will therefore have yourself believing you are being honest, so when you apply all the techniques I have shared with you, your honesty will shine through and your product will literally sell itself. The simple truth is, if you don't believe in your product, you tone of voice, hands, posture or something else will give you away.

Chapter 5 –

Surrounding Yourself with Likeminded People.

Surrounded by those that share knowledge of their success:

> *"Anyone who minimizes the importance of success to your future has given up on his or her own chances of accomplishment and is spending his or her life trying to convince others to do the same."*
> *Grant Cardone*

It is no secret that I have a close friendship with India's most famous life coach Arfeen Khan. Yes, it is in fact true that Arfeen and I speak frequently, and even when we are not physically conversing we will be in constant contact via text and email. Arfeen is a great friend. It was actually Arfeen who shared some specific advice with me, that I feel is helping me grow not only as a sales trainer but also as a person. Even though we talk often, I still watch him on 'YouTube'. Along with many other self-development coach's and motivators as it happens, people such as: Tony Robbins, Grant Cardone, Jordan Belfort, Les Brown, and Bob Proctor. In addition to which, I also read many, many books, regarding self-development, which also has propelled me forward and assisted my growth in the field of sales, but also in finding out who I am. So I feel it is fair to say that I research the type of person that I am, and I am influenced by those types of people similar to me. Those likeminded, if you will.

"Surround yourself with only the people who will life you higher"

Oprah Winfrey

My close circle of friends however, have been a much more influential and intrinsic part of making me the person who I am today. It really started to become obvious in my life about three years ago. It occurred to me back then, that I wasn't growing, personally. And it hit me; I was living the same type of life as the people who were around me. Basically my circle of friends were directly mirroring who I was, or maybe I was mirroring them. They too were essentially robbing Peter to pay Paul; living payday to payday, borrowing money from anywhere we could and even missing paying bills now and again, and attempting to make them up the month after, whilst inevitably failing to do so. Of course this meant that my personal home relationship was suffering. Even the time that I spent with my children was not as enjoyable as it should be, due to the financial pressures that come along with entertaining young people. I couldn't afford the things that other children had, and we couldn't go to the places that other children went, everything was becoming stretched.

Then one day I watched Mr. Les Brown on You Tube. I wouldn't mind but, the footage I watched was from the mid nineteen-eighties. The people in the audience were wearing the finest eighties perms and highbrow glasses. However, what time had *not* done to this footage was to have taken away the power of what that wonderful man had to say. What he said back then was as true then as it remains today. What he said was simply this: "surround yourself with powerful people" and "stay away from negative people". It struck me like a freight train, as these words rippled past his lips, and filled my ears I understood how completely correct this man was. That statement from Mr. Les Brown unravelled my problems in front of me. I took notice, quickly I moved away from those with money problems. I moved away from those that didn't want success. I moved away from those that just by their appearance created negativity. I moved towards people I wanted to aspire to become. I moved towards people that wanted to grow and develop.

"Surround yourself with positive people and you'll be a positive person."
Kellie Picker

It just so happened that during this time in my life I was working for the company DFH Financial Solutions, under a man called Charles Elliot. Charles was just the man that I could really look up to. He was everything I aspired to be. Charles was a doer, before I knew him he had left his family home of solicitors because he wanted to be a salesman. Charles never took his eye of his goals. Charles started his sales career in face to face sales, commission only.

Our beliefs about what we are and what we can be precisely determine what we can be"
Anthony Robbins

He first became the number one salesman in his office, then became number one in the country, then achieved number one status in Europe just by working hard on his dreams and skills and surrounding himself with the right people. Today Charles owns one of the UK's most popular Debt Management companies and lives a very wealthy lifestyle. I still speak to Charles, in fact I was in his office for 90 minutes last week, discussing me and my growth pattern, and sharing his stories and taking his advice. Now this is a man that clearly doesn't need me as a friend nor does he need to give up 90 minutes of his time for me, but Charles knows that I want to be successful, and that success has to be achieved ethically.

> *"Cultivate an optimistic mind, use your imagination, always consider alternatives, and dare to believe that you can make possible what others think is impossible."*
> Rodolfo Costa

There are many types of negative people in the world. Some just ruin their own lives and situations. Others however, will attempt to damage the momentum or successes of others. I personally have encountered many of these people in my time, and so have the people who I have admired; Arfeen, Charles and Hilary have all dealt with the toxic people of the world. And they, like me, have learned how to rid themselves of the influence of these toxic people from their lives. You must do too, rid yourself of statements like: "why don't you just give it up", "you can't do that" or "you're not clever enough". These are the mantras of the toxic people in the world. To succeed, we need to not hear the poison of these people, we need to block their negativity from our ears and move past their level of ability on to our own.

"Believing in negative thoughts is the single greatest obstruction to success."
Charles F. Glassman

If anyone tells me I can't do something they instantly become someone who I ignore. If they doubt my abilities, rather than encourage me to do well, our friendship is immediately over. As the saying goes, 'One bad apple can spoil the whole damn bunch', and I'm not letting anyone bring negativity to my success in life. I know it sounds harsh to remove people from my life so flippantly, but my theory is that life is far too short. Ultimately when I lie upon my death bed, and I have completed my life here, I want dearly to be able to reflect back upon what has happened in my life, and be sure that I have become all I can be, knowing that I have given it my all and nothing and no-one has stopped me from achieving what could have been done. So ask yourself: do you want to be able, to be sure, that you achieved everything you can in this lifetime? If so, you MUST do the same as me. You need to put your life before the bitterness of others and accept that you CAN be all that you want to be.

"Don't hang with negative people. They will pull you down with them.   Instead, invite them into your light and together you will both shine strong."
L.F. Young

Secrets of the Sales Master

You see the thing is, sales is not just picking up the phone or knocking on someone's front door. The truth is that, all of those people that you associate with in your personal life, will have one of two effects on the way your life develops. They will either improve or destroy your development. So, ensure you get in with the right people. Have yourself a little experiment. Pick up your mobile phone and look through the names in your contact list, and decide how many of them people in that list are positive people in your life, and how many are not. I dare you to delete the ones who are not, and see how quickly your life, and your self-confidence in your own ability skyrockets.

"Anyone that suggests to me to do less is either not a real friend or very confused!"

The harsh truth about this is that even family members should be included in your contact cull (of sorts). Family is very important, but trust me, family members can do more personal damage to your self-esteem than any 'friend' could ever achieve. Without going into too much detail and causing family issues, I will tell you that, I have a close family member who attempts to be detrimental to my self-esteem. Perhaps they do not realise they are doing it, and therefore do not do it on purpose but their negativity causes me internal frustrations and has on occasions led me to doubt myself. In actual fact there are two members of my family who have done this, and both of these to this day doubt me, or more they doubt my ambition and believe I stretch myself past my capabilities. Unfortunately the negative feedback that I get from members of my family hits me the hardest. They are the people who I love of course it does. And with them being family I would never have wanted to turn my back on them and delete them from my life. So, I tried to toe the line, and limit the amount of time I saw them at family events. Of course this was hard to do, but it is my humble opinion that without having limited contact with these specific members of my family, closer more deserving members, such as my children, would have be negatively impacted.

I cannot convey how important this particular advice is. But what I will tell you is that by doing this in my life, it immediately changed for the better. It was the acknowledgement that negativity breeds negativity. So, surround yourself with success. Sales is not an easy ride, you are going to have to work hard to succeed, and there will be tough challenges ahead of you. The simplicity of it is, you need the right advice to continue and meet the challenges head on, rather than to quit on a 'so-called' friends advice. If there is only one thing that you are going to take from this book let it be this; Build relationships with positive people that will help get the best out of you!

"Criticism precedes admiration and - like it or not - goes hand in hand with success. Keep pouring on the success, and sooner or later, the very same people who were putting you down will be admiring you for what you have done."

Grant Cardone

Chapter 6 –

Time Management

Strict time management to me is far too militarised for my liking. I am not dismissive of the importance of time management. Nor do I underestimate those who can and do work to a strict timetable. In fact I would lift my hat to them. The one thing I do understand about time management is how much time I have, and what I need to accomplish within that time to be productive and to be income producing. Funnily enough I have recently purchased a diary, however sticking to a time table is to regimental for me. I'm not saying you should not be a timetable person, it's a commonly accepted way to work in the sales industry, but for me I just know how much time I have in each day, and what I need to achieve before I finish. I am a strong believer in going with the flow to a certain point, and in doing so it opens up opportunities for me to achieve extra sales that had not been anticipated on some occasions.

So, I hear you fellow 'fly by the seat of your pants' types asking: what do you do to maintain control without the use of a schedule? The first thing I do when I arrive at the office is fire up for computer and note my goals for the day. As I have already gone over with you, the goals are the motivation, so how else should we start our day? That's right we highlight why we are here and drill it home again so imbed the enthusiasm into what we have to achieve to make them goals, reality. Next thing on the 'to do list is, the things a need to do before I go home. And, believe me this helps. Because, if I don't achieve everything on that list in that day I am painfully aware that the day after, my day will begin by completing the task's from the day before. Well that is just costing me money, the next day I should be thinking about the next days' worth of sales, not mopping up from the previous day. So simply having that list is essentially my check list to ensure I am running on time.

Now if you are choosing to adopt my Craig Faulkner, you can't whack it, impressive time management style then there are something's you need to consider; Namely, each task that you add to that to do list in the morning must be income producing, please don't be boxing out a window to go for a smoke or ring your Mrs to ask what is for tea, because that shit is not making you a single penny and it isn't part of what is important in our work day. It is a complete waste of time.

Here is a typical Craig Faulkner agenda:

- Remind myself of goals
- Clear task's from day previous (on the rare occasion I let one through the net)
- Write new list of task for today
- Call client x at 9am, as arranged yesterday

- Office Meeting at 10am, run through sales targets for the coming weeks
- Interviews at 12pm, recruitment
- Ring leads every thirty minutes
- Close at least three sales today
- Management update with partners, and direct reports
- Send emails to clients X, Y and Z confirming details/ appointment
- Call customer Y @ 5pm, as previously arranged

As you can see, it is clearly not a diary, it is simply just notes to myself. They could be more important than the examples that I have given here. But, what is important in time management is using your time wisely. It would be idiocrasy to insinuate that I never switch off in a day because I do. I like at least thirty minutes of television time, maybe a bit of golf, football or even boxing and perhaps sixty minutes of quality time with my wife and daughters. Literally finding out about their days, listening to them play, enjoying a glass of wine with the wife whilst we discuss how well our youngest daughter is doing at school or at Morris dancing. This time I treasure and it is important to have. It important to understand what my family is doing and to share in their lives. But whilst I am on the clock, during office hours, I give 110% on every single task. And, you should do the same. Why waste your time doing things half-heartedly or not producing all that you can. Never enter your office with a distraction, leave it at the door on the way in and pick it back up on the way out, once you've completed the important stuff. Remaining focused on your tasks will increase your productivity, and you will simply get more done and to a better quality with more lucrative results, believe me.

Think of it like this, you're on the phone making sales calls, your list looks like this:-

1 - Ring leads at least twice an hour,
2 - Chase current customer's information
3 - Keep current customers warm
4 - Make five sales (30 minutes each call as a minimum)
5 - Attend training session
6 - One-2-One session

If you imagine that the typical working day involves working for eight hours per day. In that day the five sales that you need to achieve to hit your target, should be take up at perhaps two and a half hours. However, before you get to those sales you need to dial the contacts, and go through a plethora of answer phones and none buyers. Along with that you have to attend training sessions, and then have a one to one as well. And all that is not mentioning, the keeping all of your customers happy with their specific requirements, calling them at specific times and to have details emailed, or in some circumstances faxed (I had one of those recently and had to dig the fax machine out of storage). Eight hours does not seem a lot anymore, does it?

The way I personally work leads me to revel at how some people can find the time to eat during a working day, never mind find time to smoke, or have a chat with a colleague about who has the biggest car. It ridiculous that some people waste valuable time fraternising when they could be generating revenue.

Increasing your productivity and working faster and more importantly, with the brevity required of each situation is very important. I could never be accused of being a 'rush the sale' type of person. In fact I am simply the opposite. Throw all your time into every sale I say, that is where the money is. But never waste time! The fact that you could be spending your time conversing with someone over the phone, about their cheque book, rather than conversing with someone over the water cooler is just a common sense approach in my eyes. No, I don't ever rush a sale, in fact the sales call is probably the most important time of the day for me. It is where most of my energies are targeted to.

What I will reveal is this: there are twenty-four hours in a day. The average person sleeps eight hours. This leaves only sixteen hours to generate. However, say two of those hours are spent travelling, two of them are spent eating, and two hours for spouse and family. You should still have an additional two hours on top of the mandatory eight hours in the office, to hit your targets. So, get in work early! Use the gift of those extra two hours to make extra money, instead of having yourself chasing your tail at the end of the week trying to scrape a target that you could have blown out of the water with a little extra push.

Consider this, millionaires such as Richard Branson and Donald Trump have the same amount in their day as you do in yours, and that I have in mine. But, what they do in their time is currently more profitable than what we are doing with our time. Perhaps the tables will turn one day and you or I will out pitch those big boys, but I can guarantee you this. You won't do it whilst sneaking outside for a smoke break, or to chat with Pauline at the kettle about her cats. Remember, success leaves clues.

> *"Long ago, I realized that success leaves clues, and that people who produce outstanding results do specific things to create those results. I believe that if I precisely duplicated the actions of others, I could reproduce the same quality of results that they had"*
>
> Tony Robbins

The trick is to work your arse off in the time that you have available to you. You have the exact same twenty-four hours that every other human being has on this planet. Know that, only by using the time you have wisely will you can create lasting success for yourself.

There is a multitude of social events that I have passed up on to commit myself to doing more at work. I have no shame in saying I will literally drop socialising like a hot potato to increase the flow of revenue within my business, to push myself to the limits. I give you my honeymoon for example. It was usurped by my career and my new wife was left seething because I prioritised career over honeymoon. The fact that she lives in a very nice house these days reconciles her somewhat as to that specific sacrifice.

It is true I work like a freaking animal, merely because I demand the best from myself, and I demand the best every single day of the week, every week of the year. You should too. Working nine to five for me is barely part-time hours. Working to those hours just limits my income to a basic. I am not now, nor will I ever be basic, and my income directly represents me, so basic is not an option. Basic wages are to pay the basic bills. Basic bills are for people who have basic lives, and basic lives are not remembered by ancestors in years to come, basic lives do not stimulate ambition in others and basic people do not aspire to succeed. Seriously why live like that?

Right now you will know if you are working your absolute hardest, and using all of your time wisely and to the best of its capability, just remember someone out there is working on the same dream and goal as you but they are probably working ten times as hard. Consider this, during the eighteen hundreds a gentleman named Stephenson created the Rocket. The Rocket was the first ever steam engine, or was it? Another inventor named Burstall, was working on a locomotive called Perseverance, but it was unable to compete in the trials and therefore lost out. It was since proven that Burstall's locomotive was a better design. Yet because he had not put the time in to be totally prepared, he lost out to Stephenson who went on to become a millionaire. The moral of the story is this: there is always someone who will compete with you. By being prepared and putting in the time you will gain the advantage over them and move forward whilst they stagnate.

I know that my peers are doing more than me right now. But I also know that I am increasing my determination every single day. Every day I make more phone calls, I have more face-to-face meetings, I send more emails, I post more social media updates. And every single day, I demand a more improved performance from myself than I did the day before.

Chapter 7 –

Stop To Think

The truth about business is that everyone who is in it, knows if they are doing enough. And what does it matter, right? Wrong... If you want to succeed in business then you need to evaluate where you are right now, what you are putting in, and ask yourself honestly; Is it enough? You'll know the answer.

Perhaps then, look around at the people you work with or those who you socialise with, how do you feel about the way they use their time? Do you think that they are all that they could be? It is okay for the purposes of this exercise to be critical of those around you; although I would advise against making any public announcements; that is if you don't wish to lose friends. You see, it is beneficial to you to pitch yourself against others, to see what it is that these people do with their lives that makes them either a success of a failure. Both sides of this agenda are equally important, as you will need to take tips from your successful acquaintances, and refrain from falling into a hole with the unsuccessful ones.

It is my solemn opinion that time is the most valuable thing we have. It is true, that as each minute of your life passes by you, that you have one less minute upon this planet, and by proxy then, one less minute to make a difference, and moreover, one less minute to succeed.

During my personal experience of life I have watched and recoiled at the wasted lives I have seen that pass me by often daily. I have often seen a homeless person sat in and about my town, and I literally shudder at what that person could have become with application, drive and ambition. I have also witnessed young women fall into pregnancy, and give up any chances of a career, seeming happy with their lot as a 'stay at home mum'; and then I compare these mums, with other mums I have met in my time. I have witnessed a personal friend of mine, after becoming a mother, then become a single mothers, then re-educate herself at university, obtain multiple employments throughout her education process to sustain her family and then go on to have a successful career in an coveted field. It seems to me, that the friend who has the drive, is the person I would wish to emulate, and that her life is more comfortable and rewarding that the friends who have embraced nappies and nursery rhymes for sustenance to their soul.

To me it is even the petty people that we meet each day that implore me to move away from them. I example the office layabout who is willing to take bathroom breaks for thirty minutes and allows their colleagues to pick up the slack for their ill behaviour, and have a 'the world owes me complex' for my part this was usually me picking up the slack, so perhaps this is mainly my bug bare. I was the one left in the office taking care of the work of three people, because my colleagues were wastes of spaces. But you know what, when them pay rises came in, and those promotions were floating about, it was me who reaped the benefits. Meanwhile, Mr. Petty Toilet Hogger, remained in his role and will probably die there on his £15k per annum. What I learned from this, was how not to be him, because like I explained before, you need to take note of both ends of this spectrum. I have no time for the like of him, *viz*, laying about in the pub every night, and spending his pittance of a wage on alcohol to sustain his negative existence. Oh yeah it may be referred to as 'the easy life' but what is easy about not being able to pay your bills, and getting divorced because you're an alcoholic and your wife is sick of not having any money coming in. Yeah that is an easy life I would rather do without.

No my esteem lies with the workers of the world, those who make a difference; service men and women, athletes, doctors, nurses, business men and women, entrepreneurs like you and I, investing in books like this to make more of ourselves and to succeed, and fight for what we believe in. The people who go the extra mile and succeed at their careers, these are the people I aspire to be like.

People like you and I are the people that run our economy. It is those of us with the ambition and drive that constitute the real governments of the world. It is you and I who run our economies. The actual Government simply set the taxes based on the drive and ethic that is set by us, the workforce.

It is the people like you and I that wake up every single day and are not only willing but that are confident in ourselves to give 100% to our causes, to give 100% to the realisation of

Secrets of the Sales Master

dreams, to give 100% of our daily exertions to filtrate the worlds revenues around the systems and sustain economic success. The fact is, that without us the governments would be truly fucked. If we the businesses were to close up shop, to remove ourselves from the system for just one day there would A, be a huge fucking melt down, but also B, there would be not a fucking thing the governments could do to prevent, sustain or resolve what we are capable of. It is 'we' who run the country, and if you want to count, then you need to be one of 'we'.

Why is it you think we have so much control, and the government do not? Because, they are not salesman like you or I. The government is not willing to go out into 'the field' face to face with their constituents, banging on doors, sometimes until their knuckles bleed, and deal with the people of the world face to face. The Government is simply not strong enough of mind or body for this work. They are

Secrets of the Sales Master

not able to pick up a phone like you and I and sell their ideas to the people. You and I have it though. You and I have what it takes to keep the world going around. To keep the money coming in. We have what it takes to charge upon industry and take it by the balls. You don't believe me? Look then to Wall Street, note then that a company's share price is based on their performance. That performance is set by the performance of their sales teams, by us!

So back to the question, are you doing enough? How much is enough? What time and effort is required to make a difference? Unfortunately, I can't put a number on that for you. But I can tell you this much, no matter how hard you are working today, you need to times it by ten tomorrow. What I mean by this is, you need to do more, you need to aim higher, and you need to give it all. Because if you're reading this book, you have already decided that you want more, you have already decided that you're willing to work for it, and if you've already decided that, then now is the time to take action and produce the new and improved you. I've said it once already, and I'll say it to you again, **success leaves clues**, use your time wisely, learn from the successes of others, and drive yourself forwards.

Chapter 8 –

Always Agree

Back to the sales process, many customers throw that common objection all salesman hate, 'Let me think about it', It is the one liner, killer or dreams right? As I look back over my time in sales I must have heard these insidious words over a million times, and even to this day I still hear that same old battle cry from clients who don't want to commit to a sale. The thing is, these days I hear it less, the reason for this is, and these words only come when I haven't done my job properly. And now when I hear them, it reminds me that I have done something wrong, and although they are still bitter to hear they now represent a reminder that I can do more, and next time I will. In essence, they are the calling card that I need to up my game again. Usually, these words will come if I've assumed that I'm getting the sale to early or

I've just been arrogant that I'm 'just that good', but this objection brings my feet firmly down to terra firma and reminds me that no one is simply that good, actually all sales come because we work for them.

So what to do, well for me I have just had the green light that I haven't tried hard enough. Something was missing from my pitch, should I abandon all hope and leave? Fuck no! This is what I do:

> I agree, 'Sir I completely agree this is something you need to think about, hey it's a lot of information to take in, but let me ask you this, on a scale from 1 to 10 where are you on purchasing this product'.

Something along these line, basically reopening the communication so I can move onto the next phase of doing my fucking job (which apparently

I hadn't done previously). Which is, back to a fact find, employ all the techniques of good sales training, building of rapport and the alike, and then when I have done my job properly I can go back and re-close the deal.

I hear it so many times where a salesperson attempts to blame the customer for a failed sale, which apparently is the outcome of these words. Sorry to burst your bubble cherub but WRONG. Correct me if I am wrong, but the client is not there to close the deal, the sales person is. If the deal doesn't close, then guess who's at fault. That's right cupcake, You! Never blame the client, that's churlish and will gain you nothing. If anything getting angry, and frustrated with your clients objection, perhaps labelling your client as 'A thick customer, who just doesn't get it' will only lead to the fracturing of rapport and a complete shutdown of this, and any future sales.

The honest truth is that you should never ever disagree with the customer. They will feel like you are kicking them in the balls. It's offensive to be blamed because you haven't been lured into a sale. If a sales person attacks you then, their attacking your intelligence 'why don't you understand that this is good for you', Really? That shit is just going to make them angry, don't do it! Instead, Agree, Agree, Agree, even when the customer is completely wrong you agree, believe me the customer will respect you for it.

Why don't you put the metaphorical boot on the other foot and ask yourself, have you ever been pitched by a salesman, or even been talking with a friend, and when you've brought up the ole 'I need to think about it' them slimy bastards had the audacity to shoot you down with a cheap challenging remark. Seriously who do they think they are challenging you, right? Yeah that is the same crap that you've been throwing at your clients. Is it really so shocking that your sales haven't been bouncing back from these encounters?

A specific example of this comes to mind. Two or three years ago an average sales call back for me was roughly 45 minutes. Now this one guy, I had already spent 90 minutes with. I have literally faced every objection in the book, it had gotten to the point where I was committed to selling that god darn product out of shear principle, on account of my valuable time that I had now already attributed to this sale. *(Just so you know the customer needed this product, so I wasn't selling them something they didn't need)* I looked at 90 minutes as 2 sales and this customer was now costing me money. However, I am a professional, and I know how easily a sale can wave goodbye if you so much as breathe an air of disagreement with a client. Not once did I ever disagree with them, all the way through the call I had that customer metaphorically wrapped up in my arms, my tone was constantly: 'I am concerned for you, but I can help you'. I never lost sight of where I needed to take this customer. Don't misunderstand me some customers will take you for a ride, and you need to sniff them out quickly. It all depends on the industry you work in. However, some customers are just scared of making that huge decision to go with you.

So remember, Agree: you will be respected for it and your closing rate will go up. Agree, agree, agree, yes sir sure sir three bags full sir, these customers need to feel heard, need to feel loved, they never, not ever, and I do mean never, need to feel challenged!

Chapter 9 –

Not Giving up!

Giving in is a bitch. It's a personal blow to your own self value isn't it? Trust me, I've been there. It is tough, and it is painful. I think it may have been the longest twenty seconds of my life sat there waiting to quit. Quit something I had started. Quit a role that I felt, at one stage, I would be good at. Walk away from something I was once so sure about. Yes, in those twenty seconds, I felt like the loneliest person in the world. And, because of how I felt then, I know that I will never ever revisit that place again in my head. However, for the purposes of this chapter I will share with you my thought process to steer clear and what it felt like!

A few years ago I had a portfolio of businesses, and working on the back of my previous success, I started a Landscaping business. It was essentially landscaping for domestic customers, who may have been looking to improve or redesign their gardens and driveways etc. It literally took off like a rocket. I couldn't believe my luck when I found that my sales were so high, literally if I got a face to face with the client, I could guarantee that 99% of my customers were signing the dotted line, bliss! Well not quite. You see, although the money was flowing in, in quick succession, it was flowing out with equal gusto. In fact it was flowing out more quickly than it came in, and for the first time in a long time, it affected my grass roots lifestyle. The household bills started to suffer, and at one stage I couldn't even pay my mobile phone bill. On paper my business had brought in £40'000 but in my pocket there was forty-two pence. For the first time during our life together, my wife begged me to quit, and even my eldest daughter Jasmin pleaded with me to listen to her mum and find another job.

Before long the debt collectors started to call, and knock on the door demanding money. I was sustaining myself on a diet of porridge and warm water. My youngest Poppy asked me for a kinder egg, and I nearly cried because I just didn't have enough money to buy my baby girl a bloody chocolate. My world seemed to be crumbling at my feet, and no matter how much work I put in, there was nothing coming back out to sustain my family.

I'm not embarrassed to say I felt like running away. Okay so maybe the twenty seconds was a mild exaggeration. I felt my world falling apart for at least a week. I felt hopeless, and powerless and a failure for what seemed like a lifetime. The fact is though, I was new to business. I was also new to self-development to an extent. But what you need to understand from this is, the reason that I am not ashamed to tell you this, is because I know you will probably, at some point, experience the same feelings yourself. But there is a solution to this black hole of doubt, and it was this that brought me away from the brink. One day in my darkest despair I had a revelation. I thought back to my days of sales training, and a specific message that had stood out to me. It stood out to me so much, that when my daughter had bad dreams as a baby, I used this message to wash away her fears and help her evolve and grow. The thought was this, What is the one thing in life that you alone, can always control?... Your thoughts! By reminding myself of this little principle at the precipice of my darkest day I was able to step away from the edge, and regain my equilibrium.

So, I decided that even though I love my wife and my children, I would continue fighting. I decided that I would work harder. I decided that I would seek solutions for the revenue I was generating, and the bills that I needed to be paid. In a time of darkness, I needed solutions…and solutions are what I was ready to find. Anyone can overcome the abyss with solutions, the goals and dreams of winners can outweigh any obstacle put in front them. This is not achieved by miracles, or divine intervention. It is achieved by the power of thought.

I addressed every issue I had in the early days of business. My beautiful wife, god I love that woman, knows that I am a fighter, and although she was scared of the situation, she believed in me, and knew I had the mental strength to pull us out of this hole. That is exactly what I did, I doubled my costs, and then I doubled my sales. My fear of overpricing is what had caused the issues, but having a belief in the product, meant that I could ask for the right price. The result, I generated enough money that I now find I am in a situation where, I could buy a brand new car every week for the next year and still be doing well financially. I'm not saying this to gloat, the reason I say this is because the power of a person's own thoughts is a powerful thing. Remaining focused is all it takes to succeed!

Another tool I used to regain my control, were the words of others. Throughout this book you will see evidence of where I draw my inspiration. But, explicitly with issues of mind over matter, I can't recommend enough the works of Arfeen Khan, more specifically: 'Secret Millionaire Blue Print'. This is the book I picked up to regain my control. It really helped me out, and prompted me to attend a seminar hosted by Arfeen. My thought process was strengthened by these words, and I found it lifted my own self-belief hearing my thoughts being made by another.

To you I say, when the tax man comes knocking or you have a cancellation or your employees leave and your wife is nagging, perhaps even your family and friends are telling you to give up! Just remember 'You control what you think, no one else' Although, most of your family and friends love you, they are not you, they cannot believe in you the way that you can, and they cannot be the voices that make you rise. So, please don't think that they mean to derail you, they care, they worry, and they love you. Accept their love, but believe in yourself.

Another example I have used in my life is Donald Trump, okay I accept he is a renowned arsehole, potential rapist, a sexist buffoon, and massive racist. But, lets us put a pin in that for the purposes of this exercise. Back in the early nineties he owed his banks Nine-Hundred-Million dollars. Nine-Hundred-Million big ones!!! (This is the kind of credit I could use in my life, right!) Regardless, that is a massif amount of cash, can you imagine what the mental pressure he must have felt, being Nine-Hundred-Million dollars in debt! Christ, some countries don't even generate that amount of money in a whole year. Then there is this dickhead, all by his lonesome, owing that much Wonga to a bank!

Shit! But, I read his book, this guys is an interesting case.... Because correct me if I am wrong, but isn't this dude now the fucking president of the United States of America? Looks like old Trumpy boy knew how to play the game. Why did he know how to play the game? Oh Right, because he believed in himself.

In his book *'Think Big and Kick Ass'* Donald states in there that he felt 'no pressure at all', none... none, he felt no pressure, no fucks were given! Really? Well that's fine, if he's telling the truth. But let be honest here, I believe he may have tossed and turned on the odd night or two, right? Regardless, look at where he is now. That guy is now worth Four Billion! Four Billion people, that's a serious u-turn. That guy literally thought he could turn it around, and he did. Mental stability, equal mega bucks.

One of my inspirational legends, Jordan Belfort, is another shining illustration of how to deal with pressure in the correct way. Belfort is that guy that who was making a million dollars a week profit. Not for his company profit, oh no, no, in his fucking pocket profit. That's serious profit right there! Some people don't make that amount of money in their entire lives. But, here is Jordan poster boy for 'the perfect life as a salesman' and why? Because he chose it, not once but twice. You see Belfort lost track of his decision making eliteness, and literally lost it all. I when I say he made bad decisions, I mean he made really fucked up decisions. Belfort in his hours of wisdomless arseholery decided to start making mistakes, first he started selling to people who didn't need what he had to offer…. Not so bad yet right? Well it is, but it gets worse. His obsession with money created a mind-set where he wanted to preserve it in the wrong way, tax evasion etc…. the guy is sliding now. Well during his slide he also consumed his body weight in drugs, and played about behind his wife's back…. Result of all these shenanigans,

Prison! Yep he went from poster boy for salesman of the millennium, to twenty-two months behind bars. This guy knows how to set the bench mark for highs and lows! Well, how did Belfort's mind rescue him from this cavernous mess? Simple, he chose to be successful, and now after his magnificent fail, he is now worth one hundred million dollars… he just chose to win!

You see mental power is something that we are all capable of. You just have to choose it. It's a drug we all have inside us called positive thoughts with physical actions, everything we do is influenced by the decisions we make. I promise you, success will not knock on your door and ask you kindly to take it. You have to beat the door of success down, you have to choose success, you have to work for success and only when you know this, only then, you will win. You will make it through any storm by focusing on the end goal!

"Never give up, for that is just the place and time that the tide will turn".

Harriet Beecher Stowe

Secrets of the Sales Master

Chapter 10 –

The Dark Days of Despair

I think the honest truth about the dark days of our lives is, we all have them. Clearly I have been there myself, and if I'm brutally honest with myself, I would have to wager that there will be more challenges in my future that will test me as a person, me as a father, and also me as a business man. You see the problem, with problems, is that all can be going swimmingly, at work, in friendships, within a relationship and even financially but before you know it, and life can be toppled over by the smallest or what may have seemed most insignificant, element of your life. The facts are; nothing can prepare you for that kind of emotional breakdown. But I guess I don't have to tell you this, you've been there yourself… right?

Yes it is all about the type of bad news that would knock any person off their feet. No one is infallible I guess. What is startling to me is that deep down I know I have worst to come, this is because my health is relatively ok right now, and when the truth is that no one gets out of life alive, you have to wager that the worst is yet to come.

Let me tell you however, about a particular stumbling block that knocked me sideways. The reason I am going into this right now is because it is flippant to accept that everyone has baggage, or everyone has had a bad day. This is not what I am inferring about. The dark days I am referring to are the days that can ruin you. Let me explain.

Sometime ago I visited my parents. I had recently been away on a business trip and life was going smoothly, as usual. My business trip had gone brilliantly, I had made some excellent contacts in Mumbai and business was taking off well generally. My home life was also going really well, wife and children made coming home a pleasure, and that's saying something for me, I'm a bit of an office-a-holic. You know I even remember that on this particular day Manchester United where playing Manchester City in a local derby match in the premier league...... things could not have been going any better for me. Literally, everything was just dropping into place like clockwork. Then sat in my parents front room, my father turned to me and from absolutely no where announced in the most candid and arguable unsympathetic manner: 'Did you know your mums had cancer, and had her breast removed!'. I swear on all my future fortunes my head just inverted. As someone who literally spends their entire life progressing at a trillion miles per hour, thinking about the move, after the move that will come after the move I felt my entire brain halt and begin to rewind. I literally could not process the information that had just been imparted to me. I was 100% out of my comfort zone and it is something I had not experienced in many years. Even in confrontations with people who I love, my mind maintains its ability to manoeuvre the situation and track a way through to a goal, but not today, not this time.

Now it is no secret that I am not really close to any of my family members even my mum. But she is still my mum and although we have really never been close, as perhaps some mothers and sons are she is and always will be the one single person in the world who I could ever love, in the way in which I love her. Okay I may not pop over for a cup of tea every other day but when the shit hits the fan, I know where I came from, I know who raised me and I know who made me into the man I am today. It's that lady in the kitchen, who now has had part of her body removed, who has been through radiotherapy and agonising treatments that is enough to shake the hardest of people, she is my mum! This may seem harsh to my dear wife, but the truth is partners can, and often do, come and go. But this is not my partner, this is my mum. I only have one, there will only ever be one, and she's been sick. But more than that, she has been sick and I was not there to hold her hand, to tell her I love her, and to stand by her.

So, my mum had had Cancer, breast cancer at that, which takes lives of hundreds and thousands of women each year. Everything that was good in my life stopped mattering, it all floated away as if it was never there to begin with. It is true when people say that their world collapses. For me it was here, at this very moment when I realised I had not only let my mum down, but I nearly lost her altogether.

My mum had been in the kitchen when my dad made his sledgehammer speech. I didn't respond to him. I'm not even sure if he said anything else, if he did I didn't hear him. I stood up from where I was sat and sought out my mum in the conservatory. I hugged her with all the love I had inside of me, and she knew then that I knew. She felt like she needed to explain to me why she hadn't told me sooner, but she didn't, I listened anyway as she explained to me that at the time she found out she had cancer, she was told that her operation would be literally the day before I flew to Mumbai. Even when, my mum was unbelievably sick, and needing me more than ever, she still put me and my children first. She knew that the deals I was travelling out there to make would be beneficial to me long term, and she felt that she didn't want to jeopardise my situation by telling me before I left about hers. She didn't want me to cancel my plans, or worry whilst I was away about her and miss opportunities. As always my mum was being the hero she has always been and putting her family's needs before her own. But, the fact remains, my mum was in hospital having surgery and I never knew. I completely understand why my mum made the decision she did, but I don't know and perhaps will never know why my dad feels that it was my fault that I didn't know.

Alas, I returned home to my wife with a streaked face, where the tracks of my tears had left in their wake a trail of hurt and sadness. I had to tell my family what had happened, and inside I felt the knots of hurt and anger growing. I just could not focus on anything other than having nearly lost my mum. As I drove down the carriageway to my house, the sun was setting and my thoughts started to wage war against themselves;

Within five days of having found out about my mum's illness, I was due to fly back out to Delhi for another two weeks of business meetings. But inside I felt internal demons preventing me from focusing on what I needed to. Instead my focus lay in doubting myself, and

I allowed everything to crumble around my feet like a house of cards, including my ability in sales. I went out to Delhi to find that I could no longer build rapport, or close a deal. I was even finding it hard to crack a smile with anyone and as a result the business trip completely flopped. Moreover, I lost friendships and contracts within days. People who just a few weeks prior I had on the end of my line, were closing the door in my face. Then I returned home to find that even business there was losing momentum and I was haemorrhaging money hand over fist. What was worse was that I had picked up a stomach bug whilst away and was laid up for nearly three weeks. I recall sitting in a bathroom at Delhi International Airport, obviously feeling very sorry for myself as I recalled where my life was just thirty days prior. I had been in the same airport, smiling from ear to ear. I had a very profitable business at home, and was opening new contacts and links with influential people in India. Life really could not have been going any better for me. But there I was on this day, a lonely shell of a man. I recollect the flight back to Manchester feeling like the longest flight I had ever experienced. I was so down, I felt so low… but, life was just about to get a whole heap worse.

Unbeknownst to me my sister had an ongoing legal battle with the father of her child parents, regarding seeking access to their grandchild. Once again my family had not made me aware of this, and I remained in the dark until it affected me personally. I myself have a daughter, who at the time of this was just five years old. As it happened the grandparents of her cousin lived just over the road from our house, and my daughter loved to spend time there. Often they would collect her from school for us, and were generally lovely neighbours who helped my wife and me out with Poppy.

Anyway, I returned home from Delhi on a Thursday, and due to my sickness I retired to bed for at least a week. During which time I engaged in a number of visits to the hospital and to the doctors. After a week I had built up enough energy to go and visit my mum, who had been my main focal point for the entire time I had been away. I wanted to see how she was doing and find out how her constant visits to the hospital where developing, and obtain a clearer picture of her situation. I walked into my mum's house to find that she was upstairs still in bed feeling quite poorly. So, I sat down to engage with my dad and get his opinion of how my mum was getting on. What I was not expecting was my dad to verbally attack me over something completely unrelated to my mother's health. My father had a problem with my daughter's relationship with our aforementioned neighbours across the street. To quote my father's closing statement; 'you, your wife and your fucking kids are no longer welcome in this house'. Well as you may understand I wanted to smash his actual skull into smithereens. This was my father, the grandfather of my daughter and he just spoken to me in this way about me his son, but moreover about my Poppy, his granddaughter. The anger and emotions pent up inside me were literally bubbling, but a voice inside interjected, and reminded me of what he had been through recently with my mum's illness, and because of that voice, I walked away. I felt sorry for him really, because I know from my own experience with helplessness, that when you are truly backed into a corner, and there is nothing you can do emotions become tangled, and logic gets off at the first available opportunity. That said, I will never forget what he said, I will never look him in the face again and not have that comment in the back of my mind. I left that day without seeing my mum. I had to. Instead, I contacted her via text message, where I asked her if I could see her when my dad was out. My mum agreed, and we arranged to meet. I didn't realise it then, but this would perhaps be the last time I would see my mum.

I arrived at my mum's house and immediately I knew something was not right, she didn't seem to me to be the mum I remembered. I don't mean that she had changed physically due to the cancer and the cancer treatment, but I mean in her mannerisms. She was very blunt when she spoke to me, and she said; 'Craig, you either stop Poppy from going round that house or we no longer want anything to do with you or your family'. She was literally that blunt. Of course I could understand my mum and dad standing by my sister. But I personally, had hardly a clue of what was going on in court. It just was nothing to do with me, and the truth is that they had hated each other for years so it was all old news to me. Literally, in one ear out the other. Regardless, after all that my mum was going through, I know I felt an illness like that would bring a family closer together. Not us, not a chance. Instead I left. I gave my mum a hug. I knew now that it would be the last time I would give her a hug. I told her that I would think things over, but we both knew I really meant goodbye.

After I left my mum's house, I went to visit my granddads grave. I still go there often, even after the ten years since his death being near my granddad provides me with a refuge where I can take the time to think about things. By his graveside just feels like a place where I can be honest with myself. I stayed there for over three hours, and ploughed through my thoughts, but the thoughts that were the most prominent at this juncture, were my memories. But more accurately, memories of my dad.

> *To call a spade a spade my dad is a racist, it is one of my earliest memories of him, which in itself it quite a sad legacy to bestow upon his child. What I mean is, its common isn't it? There really is no*

need to ignore racism, and I for one believe that highlighting it, is a step forward to eradicating it. But let us go further, my dad did more than bestow his own racist views upon me. My dad was pivotal in influencing me into being a racist. And I was, I won't lie to you, I was a horrible bigot. In fact only three or four years before I was working in India I was the most hateful racist I knew. I was literally a carbon copy of my father.

It occurred to me, whilst I was sat near my grandfather's grave that it was by stepping away from my father's views, and generating views of my own, that my life started to move forwards:

I suppose life changed for me in 2012. It was in that year that I had the absolute honour of meeting one of the most amazing women in my life. Someone who stood out from the crowd and lifted from her surrounds all that was good.

Zahra Shah is the lady I am referring to, and to this day and perhaps for all the days I have left to give, I will still love her with all my heart. Shockingly, Zahra was not a white girl from Leigh in Lancashire England! I know it's shocking right, did her name give it away? I digress, it was through Zahra that I was able to step away from a previously stereotypical view of Muslims. Zahra opened my eyes, and allowed me to engage with a multitude of nationalities without the bigoted glaze over my eyes.

Soon after I meet Zahra, I also met her husband Imran, and her sister Anum. The truth is, that it was this little family that really opened my eyes to who I had been, but more importantly who I could be. As these three people welcomed me into their lives with open arms I made friendships that would change my life, change my views and change me as a human. For their friendship I will be forever indebted, and eternally grateful.

Imran is perhaps the most genuine person that I have ever had the pleasure of meeting, and perhaps one man who I could honestly trust with my life. He quickly became a sort of father figure to me, which was alarming because on paper I had a father. Zahra was amazing also, she had special character, and a firm stance on her beliefs. She also has the warmest of hearts. I was awestruck, not in a way of attraction, but by way of friendship, I could sit and speak with Zahra for hours, or days and never become bored or distracted. Zahra, Imran and later Anum would instantly change my views on Muslims, or any other nationality for that matter. As I saw it, I had been wrong about one group of people, perhaps my general views had been flawed altogether. It was at that moment that I broke a serious rule of my father's book on life, I'd engaged with "those Muslims". But, I was learning that I had a life of my own to lead, and I was learning that maybe my dad's world view on people may not be accurate. Especially if you consider, as I saw it, it was generated from an armchair in a lowly part of England, where interaction with multicultural societies was essentially prohibited, due to the bigoted stand point of those who lived there. I decided to step away from my father's views then, and boy I'm I glad I did.

Months went by and I continued to build a fantastic friendship with my new Muslim friends. I was even visiting their home and sharing food with them. It was around November of 2012 that Anum was telling me about her fantastic uncle Arfeen Khan. Arfeen lived over in Mumbai, and he was a life coach and an entrepreneur. By this time I was already watching and reading self-help books every day; Tony Robbins, Grant Cardone, Les Brown to name a few. But I had now been introduced to this new name: Arfeen Khan. By April 2013, Zahra and Anum had told Arfeen about me and my training in sales, and I am sure they had told him about my personality too.

One Sunday evening in April at 7pm Arfeen called me, out of the blue, for a chat. For the next thirty-three minutes of my life my ambitions and my personality took on a whole new direction. Within months I was in Mumbai. Whilst there I was speaking to a crowd of over fifteen hundred people, at Arfeen's event The Secret Millionaire Blueprint. I was also meeting some amazing people, Harsh Shah, Noor Sayed, Sara Khan and so many more that I literally don't have enough ink to type.

But, the main point of this trip was that it was my first meeting with Arfeen. And it was Arfeen that really opened my eyes. We went to a Starbucks at Infinity Mall in Andheri West, and Arfeen said to me: 'So Craig, I don't know much about you but I feel like we have been friends for years' I felt immediately connected to this man, and as I listened to Arfeen for a good hour and watched how passionate he was about what he wants to achieve over the next 5 years, I felt as if it was me talking. Arfeen explained about places he would like to visit, and his life experiences and with each word I felt more and more connected to this man. Arfeen's stories had me crying with laughter, and to this day Arfeen remains one of my very best friends, and a valued friend at that. I know that if I ever need him, I just need to pick up the phone, and he will be available with friendly advice and support to help me overcome any obstacles that stand in the way of success.

All this circled through my mind whilst I was sat there in the cemetery that day. I looked to what my life was before 2012 and reflected on how it had developed into my life post 2012. The truth was that my dad despised the fact that I had Muslim friends, and the fact that I even travelled to India really got under his skin. I quickly realised that right now, I was living a life pre 2012, the life that my dad wanted me to lead. I felt I had betrayed myself by regressing this way, it felt wrong. Any decision's I was making pre 2012 was a decision my dad would make. Whereas, post 2012 I had been making the types of decisions that any normal human being would make.

I also thought about a more recent incident. Whilst visiting my parents at Christmas, my sister and my dad felt it appropriate behaviour to mock the fact that I had visited India and that I had Muslim friends. What is worse is they chose to do this in front of my two daughters and my wife. I recall how ashamed of them I felt as I watched the faces of my two daughters Poppy, 4 and Jasmin 16, as they had to sit there and endure the tirade of abuse and bigotry falling out of the mouths of their family members like vomit. They listened as their Grandfather inferred that their father was pathetic, and how I had let myself down and forgotten where I am from. This situation was then confounded as my brother went onto social media to tell Arfeen directly how, I myself in the past had been a racist.

My family now it seemed, to not only seek to embarrass me in front of my children, but they also appeared to covert the sabotage the friendships that I had made across the world, but moreover the seemed to want to actually destroy the career that I had been carving out for myself for years. Even writing this now I am reminded of the shame I feel regarding my family. If it is not bad enough that they themselves want to have bigoted views, but that they also attempted to transfer their archaic viewpoints onto my children, and simultaneously attempt to ruin my career, out of spite, hatefulness and racism.

I was disgusted by them, but still I proceeded to visit them during the year. But now, here at the cemetery it occurred to me that I had to take a stand for what I believed in. I felt like that even as a fully-fledged adult I remained to be controlled by my father and his warped views. I was being cohered into decisions because of my sister, and her ill thought out ideas regarding using her child as a weapon, rather than putting the best interests of the child to the forefront of her thoughts. So, instead I decided to stand for what I believe in. I felt that my sister was wrong! And I still do, so I decided that I would not stand by her whilst she used her child as a weapon. I went completely against my dad's wishes and remained friends with Arfeen, all of my Muslim friends, and also our neighbours across the road.

My mum said to me that she wanted to continue to see Poppy, but not me or my wife. Well, my reply to her was 'you take us as a package, or not at all'. The truth is I am pleased to break off the relationship with my father, and to a lesser extent my mum. I don't want my child in a room with a racist. I don't want her views on life to be poisoned by his incessant inability to grow up.

It upset me to turn my back on my family. It perhaps one of the greatest and most painful choices I have made in my life. But from that moment that I made my choice I felt free. I rejoiced at the idea of not hearing my father tell me how pathetic I am. I was elated to consider that my children would not be subjected to a poisonous Christmas party of abuse, with all the fun sucked out. I was now free to move on with my life, to engage with anyone I chose and I felt like a new person again. Within days I was able to refocus on work, and I hit the ground running, picking up the pieces and restructuring the plan to be bigger and better than it ever was before.

I think of my mum often, and what she must be going through, but my life is my life, it won't be dictated by others views. Hopefully, one day she will contact me and say, 'Craig, I'm sorry and I am proud of you'. If I ever hear those words from my dad, then I will have achieved what I have set out to do, and I would go to my grave a contended man. But, for now I deal with the challenges that life throws at me. I've learned from this that I should never get too comfortable. Life can hit you hard, and next time it may hit me harder than it has before. Last time I was down for months, but I managed to dust myself off, pick myself back up and reassess my goals. The fact is, winning is not about how many times that you are knocked down, or how fast and painful those blows come at you. To be a winner, is about how you pick yourself back up, and how to mentally prepare yourself to continue to pick yourself back up. I may have been down for longer than normal, but I found myself willing to take that next step and move forward. You too will face huge challenges I'm sure, in fact I know you will. However, just remember that I have been there, and so has countless others. Some of who have had more difficult times than me or you no doubt, but we all kept on going. I'm just a lad from a small town called Leigh in Lancashire, I have a broad accent, and I like the occasional drink. There is nothing special about my life, or my background that makes me more suitable to overcome adversity. What I am saying is, if you have the drive to be up there at all, then you have the drive to get back up there if you fall. I'm just like you. I stand by this saying; *'If life creates the problem, life creates the solution'*.

Secrets of the Sales Master

Secrets of the Sales Master

Chapter 11

Willing to go the Extra Mile

In my career I have always been one of those people who were willing to take it to the next level. Some people during my time have commented on my behaviour as being something negative; they are so wrong. The truth is I have often perused my peers and observed the 'Just a Job' crew. You'll know them, the ones that turn up to work to merely work their nine to five shift, to then go home, feeling like they've done a day's work. My friends I hope for your sake, this isn't you. I dare say there are some of you who have experienced this mental block, and it is a mental block, and maybe even some of you who are currently in this place. Get out, run, run as fast as you can away from this nonchalant mindset, it's a killer of dreams and a ruin of the most promising careers.

Instead think of your situation from a difference perspective. Imagine yourself as the owner of a business, and ask what you would expect from your staff, and who you would reward. My guess is that you would be looking to promote the doers, over the nine to fivers, right? Moreover, would you really think to yourself that after achieving, a nine to five status, that you would be anywhere close to the top one percent of achievers in your industry. In fact why don't you conduct an experiment? Find out who the highest achievers are in your field, and then observe their working hours. I assure you they won't be slight.

Come on, let's face the truth of this situation, if you're putting in the extra hours, you will be at the absolute minimum teaching you the valuable lesson that a nine to five wage, pays nine to five bills. If you want the bonuses of life, you need to achieve the bonuses of business, and that can only be done by moving past the mundane. So reflecting back to your own life; how many people do you witness jetting off to some paradise holiday, after putting in four, six, even ten hours of overtime a week? That's right, they knew how to play the system and it's working for them. The rewards are being reaped.

Similarly, look to, how many sales people do you see just falling short of their target and start complaining that the target is unachievable? These are the ones who start to beg their manager to pay out even though they've missed the target, yeah right that seems like the way a business is going to make its money. These kinds of people disappoint me in a big way, I know that sounds harsh but it's true. Sales is an opportunity, it not a job and if someone is working at a job in sales they're quite honestly missing the opportunity of sales.

Now, I say opportunity because, in the sales environment it is you, and only you, that is capable of granting you, a pay rise. It is only you who is capable of smashing a target; it is only you who has the opportunity to take it to the next level. Now I appreciate that skills must be acquired, that is why I am here. But, it's you who has to implement these skills commit to the matter at hand and take it to the next level. But then when you have learned these skills, you will witness that the rest of your life can be positively affected by these skills, and moreover your winning attitude will assist you in creating other opportunities that you never thought you even deserved.

Take my situation for instance, I honestly believe that if you were to speak to old school friends, or even my family members about me, or better my old school teachers and ask them; if Craig Faulkner had the drive, ambition and confidence to speak on stage to hundreds of people, all because he had learned what it takes to persuade and influence, I don't believe a single one of them would agree. I know certainly that many would doubt the changes that are possible, from the acquirement of sales skills. I honestly believe that the person I was, would cloud their judgement of the person I am now, and that they would have assumed a less productive life for me. Well I showed them, right? Well my friends, come join me, show your doubters the person you are capable of being, rather than the person they assume you are.

I have worked seven days a week since leaving school, but the thing is, only in the past five years have I really started to work in the right areas. I've done this, by focuses my efforts with the right type of learning. Learning for me is to look to the people I aspire to be and to take notice of their lessons. Some influential names to me have been Grant Cardone and Jordan Belfort. Their lessons these men have shown me, that the effort that I have within me, is the only thing that is going to elevate me to the next level. And when I'm not learning I'm doing. As an aspiring entrepreneur I commit my time, and some, to doing my utmost to make a difference, every single minute of the day.

One key aspect of my learning experience is increasing the amount of effort I put into everything, every day. The calls I make, the people I speak to, the books I read; the truth is that I am on a mission to learn. I have a strange feeling, that what I put into this life will affect me in the next. Deep right! But many spiritual doctrines believe that what you put into this life, you take with you in the next. So my aim is to learn all I can, and then when I enter the next version of me, I won't have so far to peddle, and their won't be as big of a void between where I start, and reaching my dreams.

As a frequent passenger on airlines, I am able to afford a great deal of time to the acquirement of knowledge, so every time I jump on a plane, I grab a suitable book and engage with the text as best I can to not only read the words, but absorb the information. A few years ago I travelled to Tunisia for a vacation. Whilst there I read the same book three times. It was called: *Millionaire Upgrade*. I imbedded the principles of the book into my brain, and I'm considerable richer now, so I dare say it did me good. What I am saying is read, read, read….Books are a gift, they are the successes, and failures of others, and you can learn so much from books.

I understand that some of you may have families, and relationships that you are dedicated to, well that's okay. But remember that you are working for your family, not against it. If you find yourself in a confrontation with your other half over how much you work, well I am afraid it's times to sit that person down and explain to them the bigger picture. Make your family part of your dreams, and by that I mean explain to them the importance of dreams, of success and share your life with them. Have your very own cheerleading squad at your side, and allow them to engage with the success too. I love bringing my daughter into the office, and she loves it too. Poppy is seven now, and has already put a head-set on for the phones. But more importantly than her having the experience of being in the office, she sees that her father is respected by his team. She can reflect that respect and appreciate what it is that I am working towards, because she sees how others see me, and understand that what I am doing is not a waste of time but a career, worthy of respect. She witnesses first-hand the effort that I put in, and enjoys the idea of business. Even at home, she has learned the telesales pitch, and on one occasion she even had insight into a pitch to a customer.

Only recently my older daughter Jasmin, twenty, has come to me and said:

> "Dad, I know I've complained to you over the years by not being around that much, and even complained when you go to India. But, I've finally realised that you do all this for your family. I really want to be like you and work really hard on my own goals and dreams. I realise now, that there are people out there that do whatever they can to hold you back and stop you from growing as a person. You have faced so many challenges and you don't let anything stop you from doing what you want to do!"

I have to admit, I was holding back the tears, I never told Jasmin that but it made me feel immensely understood, and proud having heard that from her. It means so much to be recognised by your children, and have them understand that your dreams are worth their pride.

Today my amazing daughter Jasmin, starts her own career; working with people who have learning difficulties. She is an amazing young woman, with such a warm heart. I understand my daughter, I know that she will go on to do amazing things in her life and the reason I know this, is because, she does makes her smile, seven days a week. Going the extra mile requires serious commitment, not just a couple of days or weeks or even for a couple of months. Going the extra mile requires continual commitment for the rest of your life. Only you can really decide whether or not if you have that drive and determination inside you. If you don't have it, if you're not fully prepared to engage with all you have, for the rest of your life, put this book down and choose different career, because sales is not for you!

Chapter 12

Finances

Five years ago there would have been no way what so ever I could give you any advice in this department. Literally as soon as I had money, I spent it! It was almost as if I was allergic to the touch of money in my hand, so I had to get shot of it immediately and spend it on crap I dare say I didn't need. Money would just fly out my bank account within hours of it arriving there. I literally blew thousands upon thousands of pound on shite! I have always blamed my schooling for that. I mean seriously, why is it schools do not teach children about money management? They can tell you the angle of a set of ladders against a wall, based on the length of the ladder and the height of the wall, but not how to balance your pay check. I'm still waiting to learn how trigonometry is going to affect my life…. Ever! Anyway, back in my early years I ran up huge credit cards bills, loans upon loans, overdrafts, mortgaging the house, you name it, and I blew the lot!

Today however, I treat money like I treat my children. I look after it, I invest it. I don't keep money in my bank account, I see that as dead cash lining the pockets of the bank managers of the world. No instead I invest in a number of different things. Of course, I hold enough cash back to live on, to support my lifestyle, my family and ensure that life's little necessities tick over all tickerty boo. But, the money that I have invested, is what counts, because that it what will one day make me a very wealthy man.

With this I tend to keep my feet firmly on the ground. I do not posit that I am something I am not. I feel I don't need to lord my wealth over people, so I tend not to be over flash about what I have. My roots, are a council estate in the north west of England, and to be respectful of what I have without having to besmirch others with my wealth seems to be a more grounded lifestyle for my children to learn from. I always think, money doesn't make a person good or bad, even the poor can be good people, do what's the point in showing off your wealth, and it doesn't make you a better man, merely a richer one. Still, I remember the feeling of payday when I was in financial instability. Especially when payday was monthly. I would literally live for one weekend like a millionaire, and then by money, I hardly had the finances to buy a bus pass, to get my arse back to work for the next month, or buy a sausage roll for my lunch.

So, why did my view on money change? Well, it's simple really, my social circle changed. Once again I return to my mentor Arfeen Khan, a wan who I have taken so much wisdom from, learned so many of life's lessons, and a man who I will go to my grave being forever indebted to. You see when I met Arfeen, I changed my social circles. I moved from being like-minded with people who blew their money as soon as they'd earned it; to being like-minded with people who saved, invested and gave sold and strong advice to me. I understand that I can't take my wealth into the next life with me. In fact I have an aim to leave my wealth to a number of children's charities. The truth is my children will earn their own money, and would respect the charities receiving the money, over themselves, because that is how I have raised them.

The point is, it is massively important that you also really get to grips with your own finances. Money literally can be like gold dust, and seep through your fingers before you realised it had ever been there. What you do with your wealth is your choice, but at least generate it before you make that choice. Your wealth is part of your growth as a person. Now it is your time to become responsible. It is your time to rise.

Secrets of the Sales Master

Let Your Journey Begin

Secrets of the Sales Master

Thank You, to those that have been a part of my journey, and those that have motivated me to produce this book.

Firstly, I just want to thank my good friends, **Zahra and Imran**. The both of you have been a huge support to me from the very first day that we met. I will always hold a special place in my heart for you both, and I hope to spend many more years bringing smiles and love to your warm hearts.

To my wife, **Sarah-Jane**. There are not enough words to fully articulate how much you mean to me. You are my soul, my love and my life. Thank you for holding your head high when times were hard. Thank you for supporting me, and our children through the dark days. You are now, and always have been my better half. I love you for always, and I am so proud to call you my wife.

Arfeen Khan, my friend, my mentor. Thank you for your words, your wisdom, and your friendship. You will always be the man that I inspire to be. Your commitment to helping others and sharing your ideas and dreams is something I truly admire.

To the lady of a thousand and one words, **Kate Matthews**, Well you are a legend! Thanks for keeping the book on track, for dealing with my shit, and helping me to understand how to be a better author. Thank you for your knowledge, and insight. And, here is to our next project together.

Danny Rich, Thanks for your friendship and dedication to improve your abilities and sharing those ideas with me.

To *My Mother*, thank you for being my first love. You brought me into this world, and cared for me. It is to you I owe my life, and I thank you from the man I am today, I owe it all to you!

I want to thank *My Dad* for motivating me to produce this book. You know what you did. And, it's because of you, that I am a better man.

Steve Kerrigan, someone I have only known such a short space of time, but your work ethics and determination to produce results keeps me pushing for the next success.

I want to thank everyone at *Renewable Solutions Team* and *One Nation Energy*, Owners *James & Karen Mclaughlin*,
Your belief in me, and your trust in my ability is profound. I am proud to be the Director of Operations at your companies. I hope together we can grow the businesses to become a household name.

Secrets of the Sales Master

Hilary Madeley, without you this journey would never have started, you mean so much to me, and I will never forget your dedication and friendship, I thank you for believing in me so early on in my career, you will always have a special place in my heart.

Finally, I want to thank three *special* ladies in my life, my girls **Poppy** and **Jasmin**, and a lady very close to my heart **Abbie Ostrowski**.

Poppy for your smile, for your love and for you five minute hugs, I thank my lucky stars each day. You are my princess. Thank you for making your daddy smile. You are the one person that keeps me level headed, and I only need to see you smile to lift me in tough times.

Jasmin, you are my daughter. There are no steps in my heart. I dedicated this book to you, because you make me proud, you make me strive and I am honoured that you allow me to be your father. From the moment I met you I loved you, and you make me so proud of you, every day.

Abbie, it's an honour for you to call me your un-official father. I want you to know that allowing me to be a father-figure to you has made me so very proud. My dedication to your love will be forever impenetrable, for you are one of my girls.

I am enchanted at how mature and hardworking you are, especially at such a young age. You and Jasmin are so alike. And, whilst your dad is no longer with us, I know he would be so proud of you, because my eyes see what a father eyes should see in you, and I am always, so proud.

www.ingramcontent.com/pod-product-compliance
Lightning Source LLC
Chambersburg PA
CBHW061646040426
42446CB00010B/1611